The Complete Studio Guitarist

The Guitarist's Guide to Session Work and Home Recording

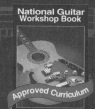

National Guitar Workshop Book

Approved Curriculum

VIVIAN CLEMENT

Alfred, the leader in educational publishing, and the National Guitar Workshop, one of America's finest guitar schools, have joined forces to bring you the best, most progressive educational tools possible. We hope you will enjoy this book and encourage you to look for other fine products from Alfred and the National Guitar Workshop.

ISBN 0-7390-3536-3 (Book & CD)

This book was acquired, edited and produced by Workshop Arts, Inc., the publishing arm of the National Guitar Workshop.
Nathaniel Gunod, managing and acquisitions editor
Ante Gelo, music typesetter
Timothy Phelps, interior design
CD recorded by Anthony Paiano at Exodus Studio, Mississauga, Ontario, Canada
Interior photographs by Stella Jurgen, 17 Designs, Missis...

D1411188

Alfred

TABLE OF CONTENTS

A compact disc is included with this book. The symbol shown at the left appears next to every example that is on the CD. Use the CD to help ensure that you're capturing the feel of the examples and interpreting the rhythms correctly. The numeral below the symbol corresponds directly to the CD track number. Track 1 has a brief introduction and Track 2 provides tuning notes for the guitar.

ABOUT THE AUTHOR

Vivian Clement is a versatile guitarist whose style ranges from jazz and blues to pop and rock. She studied jazz with Peter Harris at Humber College in Toronto as well as vocals with classical/pop teacher Helen Knight. Vivian owns and records at Exodus Studio with her husband Anthony Paiano. She has taught guitar at the National Guitar Workshop. She keeps busy performing in the Southern Ontario region, teaches privately and has released several CDs.

ACKNOWLEDGMENTS

I'd like to thank the following people: Nat Gunod, Donna Grantis, Dave Schaufele, Andrea Mathew, Chris Gormley, the Cavallo family and David Norris-Elye. Special thanks to Tony Paiano, Rob Hoinkes, Caroline Edwards and Dianne Ticknor.

INTRODUCTION

This book assumes you have a general knowledge of music theory, basic chords, reading standard music notation, tablature and scales. It is about being a studio guitarist and putting together a home studio.

Although you can earn a lot of money being a studio guitarist, and it provides a more pleasant working environment than being on the road or playing in smoky rooms, it does require quite a bit of skill and diversification. Top session gigs seem to be reserved for the elite veterans who possess superior chops, sight-reading skills and years of experience. In big name studios—where artists' careers are at stake—large overheads and big budgets don't allow for unknown newcomers. The same is true for doing jingles for national ad campaigns and composing or playing for movie soundtracks. Producers are not willing to take chances on the new kid on the block, and seasoned players are inclined to protect their positions in the business.

But there is no need to despair. There is still a lot of work available on a smaller scale for local jingles, songwriting demos and independent films as well as corporate videos. Thankfully, the vast majority of session work is in this arena. Image, which is an important aspect of performance on a gig, is replaced by good sight-reading skills and access to a broad palette of sounds and styles. Having the appropriate gear, a good attitude and being a team player are all important elements of being a successful and employable guitarist.

Being a studio musician is all about creating great music for someone else to enjoy, but it can be just as enjoyable as creating music for yourself. And who knows, perhaps as you hone your guitar skills you will be able to climb the echelons of the studio/music business.

Parts 1 and 2 of this book cover important aspects of what you need to know for a career as a studio musician. Topics include appropriate gear, developing a great sound and having a professional attitude in the studio. Also covered are topics such as chart reading and building interesting licks from scales. In addition, different styles of music are discussed. This section will help "fill in the gaps" for players who have done some session work but want more information.

Part Three is about setting up a home studio for basic recording. It covers topics such as the importance of computers as well as multi-track recording, and shows you how to put together a great demo.

It's a good idea to apply what you learn from this book in a working environment or in your own home studio as soon as possible. The knowledge you gain will only become solidified once you put it into practice.

PART 1—GEAR
CHAPTER 1
GUITARS AND GUITAR ACCESSORIES

Let's discuss the equipment you will need to be a successful studio musician.

Walk into any local music store and you will find the walls decorated with various types of guitars ranging from inexpensive beginner guitars to expensive, ultra-professional guitars. There will usually be a few sections for guitars: one with a selection of acoustic guitars and the others with different types of electric guitars.

The music market is flooded with new products and new styles of guitars are added every year. Although different types of electric guitars have been with us for many decades, they all fall into only a few categories: solid body guitars with single-coil and/or double-coil pickups, and hollow body guitars. Of course there are many variations of these guitars. We will be covering the most popular types of guitars.

Most music stores carry many styles of electric and acoustic guitars ranging from inexpensive to very pricey.

There really is no single electric guitar perfect for use in all recording situations. It's all a matter of preference and experience, and most of all, developing your own great tone. Throughout your career, you will go through many different types of guitars. When you are hired to record, you will be expected to have a basic collection of guitars from which to choose.

THE SOLID BODY (SINGLE- AND DOUBLE-COIL PICKUP GUITARS)

There are three types of solid body guitars: those with only single-coil pickups, ones with only double-coil pickups and hybrid guitars with both kinds.

There is a distinct difference between the sounds of single-coil pickup versus double-coil pickup guitars. Single-coil pickups make a bright, clean sound while double-coil pickups are associated with a big, dark sound. Many studios and gigging musicians own a variety of both. In order to be well equipped and ready for the studio, you should start with owning one double- and one single-coil pickup guitar.

Single-coil Pickup Guitars	Double-coil Pickup Guitars
Fender Stratocaster	Gibson Les Paul
Fender Telecaster	Paul Reed Smith guitars

If your budget doesn't allow you to own one of each and you presently own a guitar with single-coil pickups, you could replace one of the pickups with a double-coil (or vice versa), creating your own hybrid. Or, purchase a hybrid. There are plenty of hybrids to choose from that already have both single- and double-coil pickups built in.

The key is in understanding the difference in the sounds and to know which sound is needed for a particular project. Some musicians tend to go a little overboard, spending all their hard-earned cash buying all the newest guitars and products that come on the market. This would, no doubt, make your local music store very happy, but owning just a few really good, versatile instruments (and other basic gear) should suffice to get you started. As you progress you can expand your collection, adding different types of guitars as you feel you need them.

Guitarists have a tendency to favor one particular guitar over another, especially if they have been playing one particular style for a long time. For example, if you are an R&B or old-school funk player and a lot of your gigs are in this style, chances are you own a guitar with single-coil pickups. But once you start doing studio work, you will quickly begin to realize the importance of also owning a double-coil pickup guitar. At some point you will be hired to play in styles requiring beefier and fuller sounds.

There are a lot of guitarists who use rackmounted effects to enhance their sound and make their single-coil pickup guitar sound darker and richer like a double-coil pickup guitar. With all the modern technology that is now at your disposal, you can buy pretty realistic sounding digital amps and rackmounted effects enabling you to reproduce almost any guitar tone known to man.

Some musicians would rather depend solely on their pickups and use pedals with an amp to get the exact sounds they desire. These players are usually not huge fans of the digital sound and feel that the truest and purest tones come from actually using the right guitar for the right sound. It all comes down to your own personal taste and what you find works best (more on this in Chapter 3 of this book). The best situation is to actually own a double-coil pickup guitar, since it is difficult to reproduce that sound any other way. Combined with a great amp, a double-coil pickup guitar can easily create the great distortion that is so frequently used in rock and alternative songs.

The important thing is to understand which music is more suited for a single-coil versus a double-coil pickup guitar. Experience, and using your ear, will determine what you will need for each style of music.

Technical Tip No. 1—Custom Pickups

If you are unhappy with the tone of your guitar, try installing new pickups. Replacement pickups can change the tone of your guitar quite dramatically. Seymour Duncan, DiMarzio and Schecter are a few companies that offer replacement pickups.

You can replace single-coil with double-coil pickups (or vice versa) to create more versatility in sound, although you may be well-advised to get a guitar tech to install them.

Left-handed guitarist playing single-coil guitar.

THE SINGLE-COIL PICKUP GUITAR

Single-coil pickups are commonly associated with Fender Stratocaster or Telecaster guitars. They are bright and clean sounding.

STUDIO TIPS FOR USING SINGLE-COIL PICKUPS

When you are called to do a studio session, the person hiring you will give you details on which type of guitar they are looking for. It's not necessary to own every guitar, but it's vitally important to have a good grasp of how to reproduce the sounds being requested. At times, the only information you may have is that you will be laying down a guitar track for a pop artist. The key to being confident and successful in the studio is to listen to a lot of music in all styles. This will enable you to become familiar with the various sounds used for any style of music. Like any skill you want to acquire, this takes an investment of time. It will be time well spent, since you never know when you will be called upon to play a particular type of music.

For example, let's say you've been hired to lay down a track for a country song. There is a high probability that the producer or artist is going to want to hear a single-coil pickup sound. Country music guitar sounds are usually very bright and twangy, and people normally want that sound for that style. In some of the new country-rock tunes, distortion effects are used to play heavier sounding power chords, but the standard single-coil sound still prevails.

> ### Technical Tip No. 2—EQ
>
> *Setting up EQ (equalization) for your electric guitar is a very important step in getting a great tone. You can use the EQ on your amp, a pedal or a rack-mounted EQ. For the best results, set your EQ around the following frequencies.*
>
> *1. Low end around 100Hz**
> *2. Mid from 500Hz to 600Hz*
> *3. High end from 3kHz** to 4kHz*
>
> *Experiment with these frequencies to find where your tone sounds best for you. In the lower end, if you get too close to 200 Hz your guitar may sound muffled and lack clarity. In the midrange, you need to avoid a boxy, AM radio sound. In the high end of the spectrum, be careful of getting too piercing a sound.*
>
> **Hz = Hertz. The frequency rate of soundwaves.*
> ***kHz = Kilohertz. 1,000 Hertz.*

If you've been hired to play rhythm guitar, it doesn't hurt to inquire if you will be adding any acoustic or lead guitar to the tracks. This will allow you to bring suitable equipment and be ready for the session. Either way, it is best to arrive prepared with a few guitars just in case the producer or artist decides they want something different than what was originally requested. Sometimes a song takes a different turn than anticipated. Having that extra instrument can be the determining factor for the direction the song will take. It also makes you look professional and flexible if you are always willing to go the extra mile for whoever is hiring you. Since there is a lot of competition for studio work, it doesn't hurt to cover all your bases.

Other styles of music that usually use a single coil pickup sound are R&B, blues, reggae, soul, funk and many types of rock.

CHALLENGES OF SINGLE-COIL PICKUP GUITARS

One of the challenges of recording with a single-coil pickup guitar is the hum the pickups can generate. If you have this problem, you may be situated too close to the amp. The best way to eliminate this noise is to move the guitar in different directions until the hum stops. Some studios will have the amp in a completely different room from where you are playing and provide headphones so you can hear yourself and the rest of the music. This is usually because a very high amp volume is needed to get the desired sound. If the amp is not in proximity to your pickups, the noise should stop. If you are still getting a hum once you are away from your amp, look around to see if you are close to any light source or computer monitors. Usually your engineer is aware of these potential problems, but it depends on his or her experience.

In most studios, the amplifier is put in another room to isolate the sound and avoid noise interference.

It's a good idea to start collecting albums of artists who play various styles of music on single-coil guitars. Spend time listening to their tone and do research through books, magazines or the Internet on the type of gear and accessories they use to get their signature tones. Try and imitate their sounds and be ready to produce it if it is needed during a session. Below is a list of popular guitarists who play single-coil guitars.

SUGGESTED LISTENING FOR SINGLE-COIL PICKUPS

Eric Clapton	Eric Johnson
Buddy Guy	Bonnie Raitt
Jimi Hendrix	Stevie Ray Vaughan

Double-Coil (Humbucker) Pickup Guitars

The word "humbucker" is synonymous with double-coil pickups, and rightly so because they cancel the humming effect created by single coils. A double-coil pickup is comprised of two side-by-side single-coil pickups. The two coils are wired out of phase (meaning the crests of the sound waves from one align partially with the valleys of the waves from the other, creating a canceling effect, see page 86), which is how they eliminate the hum. If you are looking for more power and a fuller, punchier sound, double-coil pickups are what you need.

The double-coil pickup guitar has a very different sound than its counterpart, the single-coil pickup. The former is warm and dark sounding while the latter is bright and twangy. Humbuckers also respond differently to the application of distortion: a single-coil pickup tends to acquire a bright, loose sound while the double-coil pickup attains a tighter, fuller sound.

A lot of heavy rock guitarists use double-coil pickups to get the great, warm distortion so commonly used from the 1970s onward. These guitars have a natural sustain that comes from being designed with a heavier wood.

Recording sessions requiring a double-coil pickup will probably be in the styles of rock, heavy metal, alternative rock or blues (although a lot of blues players use single-coil pickups to get more bite and brightness). Many alternative rock bands use double-coil pickup guitars since they sound great with distortion pedals or distortion coming from an over driven amp, such as a Marshall cabinet. You could also use this guitar for recording fusion or progressive rock.

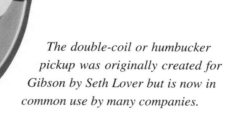

The double-coil or humbucker pickup was originally created for Gibson by Seth Lover but is now in common use by many companies.

Double-coil pickup guitars are usually constructed of heavier woods, which create a long, natural sustain. They have a chunky, rich tone.

Spend some time at your local music store trying out different guitars. Try playing a Les Paul, which has very rich tones, and compare it to a Telecaster. You will immediately hear the difference between the two. Look around for different makes and models. You should also try playing hybrid guitars, which have both a single- and double-coil pickup, to hear how they compare with other guitars.

One thing you can do is rent a few guitars from a music store. While this may seem a little impractical, there are invaluable lessons to be learned from having time to experiment with the sounds of different guitars. This will also make it easier to discover flaws that are not immediately apparent from a quick test in the store.

You will find that although some guitars are very comfortable while sitting down, they are cumbersome and awkward when standing. The opposite also applies: there are guitars that are well-balanced and great for standing but feel unbalanced and unstable when seated. Feeling uncomfortable during a long session can create fatigue, which would ultimately hinder your creativity.

You will begin to discover the difference between inexpensive and well-built, pricey guitars. Once you've played a well-constructed, great sounding guitar with a great neck and feel, it will be difficult to see yourself playing anything less. Although you may not be able to afford the best right away, you can always trade in your present guitar and make monthly payments on a better one. It would be well worth the investment; it's the industry standard that musicians own professional instruments.

If you can't afford the cost of a rental, try borrowing a guitar from a friend for a few weeks in exchange for one of your own guitars. This is an inexpensive way to analyze different guitars.

> ### *Technical Tip No. 4—Controlling Distortion*
>
> *Once you have the distortion set for your guitar (either with a pedal or rack-mounted effect) you can control it by rolling back the volume of the guitar until you get the desired result. This allows you to add or lay back on your distortion in different areas of a song rather than having to do it manually from the device.*

An excellent exercise is to have someone play through the changes of a song with a double-coil pickup while someone else solos using a single-coil. Then, reverse the roles. The solo from the single-coil will usually "stick out" a little more since it has more treble and therefore more of a cutting edge. Playing chords with a single-coil will sound a little thin. On the other hand, the double-coil strumming will be thicker and fuller but it will not cut through so much during a solo because of its darker sound. This is a good test for hearing how the two types of guitars perform in different roles.

STUDIO TIPS FOR USING DOUBLE-COIL PICKUP GUITARS

The biggest problem you will encounter with double-coil pickups is in the area of EQ. Since humbuckers are duller sounding, your guitar track can get buried in the mix (especially if you are using distortion). This problem is more apparent in the high end but is easily solved by using a good EQ to brighten up the sound. If you have a good idea of what type of tone you like, it shouldn't be too hard to reproduce in a studio setting. (You may have to do some tweaking if you are going through the studio's effects rather than your own).

CHALLENGES OF DOUBLE-COIL PICKUP GUITARS

Although a humbucker pickup makes less hum than a single-coil pickup, there are other concerns you may encounter in the studio. For example, a double-coil pickup produces a lot more sound at a lower level. This is because humbuckers are wired together in series, which increase their power. Make sure you don't have your amp volume turned up too high, or it may be difficult to get a clean sound—particularly if you have a tube amp. (If distortion is what you are after then by all means crank it up). Also, if you are overdriving your amp to get distortion, you will definitely need to isolate it in a different room due to the high volume. This is something your engineer should know about, however, you should be familiar with the settings on your amp and guitar to get the sounds you are after.

SUGGESTED LISTENING FOR DOUBLE-COIL PICKUPS
Carlos Santana
Eddie Van Halen
Steve Vai

HOLLOW BODY ELECTRIC GUITARS

There are two types of hollow body guitars: the standard hollow body and the semi-hollow body. Hollow body guitars are not as popular as solid body guitars, but at some point you will probably find yourself in a situation where one is needed. Some hollow bodies have single-coil pickups (such as the Gibson ES-150 used by jazz guitarist Charlie Christian) but they usually come with humbuckers. This is because these instruments are usually used for jazz and/or swing, where the darker sound is appropriate. However, some of the early rock 'n' roll players, such as Chuck Berry and Freddie King, also used this guitar.

Even though hollow body guitars generally have double-coil pickups, they sound quite different than double-coil solid body guitars. Their distinct sound is the result of the body being hollow and wide. This kind of guitar has less sustain than other electric guitars. A hollow body has a round, mellow tone, which lends itself well to jazz. Since you can't really reproduce its sound using any other guitar, it is a necessary part of a complete guitar collection.

Studio Tips for Using Hollow Body Guitars
Hollow body guitars are played mostly by blues and swing guitarists. Many guitarists use them for jazz chord/melody playing. Even though hollow bodies are associated with specific styles of music, you may be asked to use one now and then simply for its unique sound.

Hollow body guitars usually have double-coil pickups but are a little brighter than solid bodies with double-coils. They have a woody, round sound.

Technical Tip No. 5—Finger Noise

When either electric or acoustic guitar are recorded, finger noise (the sound of the fingers moving up or down the strings) is often a problem. This may be caused by sloppy technique, in which case you'll have to learn to play more cleanly. It may also be the natural result of playing a quick passage. If this becomes a problem, you can simply apply a small amount of cooking oil to the strings and wipe off the excess with a cloth. This will eliminate a lot of the noise. Unfortunately, you will also be changing your strings more frequently, since the oil takes away a lot of the brilliance. Using flat wound strings, which are also less brilliant, is also a solution.

SEMI-HOLLOW BODY GUITARS

These guitars came from the fuller-bodied "electric-acoustic" hollow bodies. They were first manufactured by Gibson in the 1950s to diminish the problem with freedback. One of the popular semi-hollow body guitars is the Gibson ES-335, which has been successful since the 1960s. Even today, many popular guitarists play them.

There is a lot less sustain from a semi-hollow body since the body is thinner than a hollow body. Many manufacturers have been able to increase sustain by placing a solid piece of wood in the center of the body.

Hollow bodies were also called "semi-solid" or "thin-bodies" in the 1950s. Most have f-shaped holes and wood in the center of the body to avoid feedback.

CHALLENGES OF HOLLOW BODY AND SEMI-HOLLOW BODY GUITARS

Many hollow body and semi-hollow body guitars come with F-holes (f-shaped holes located on the top of the body). Because of this, particular care must be given to the volume, as they tend to produce feedback if cranked up too loud. In most contexts that are appropriate for a hollow body, your volume will be low enough that feedback will not be a problem.

SUGGESTED LISTENING FOR HOLLOW BODY GUITARS
George Benson
Chuck Berry
B.B. King
Tal Farlow
Barney Kessel
Pat Metheny
Wes Montgomery
Brian Setzer

ACOUSTIC GUITARS

STEEL-STRING ACOUSTIC GUITARS

In the 1990s, there was a resurgence of interest in the steel-string acoustic guitar, mostly thanks to the alternative music scene. During the 1980s, the acoustic guitar had all but disappeared from the popular music scene, but then became the trademark of many alternative musicians.

If you don't presently own an acoustic guitar, you need to purchase one because at some point you will surely be called to lay down acoustic tracks. This instrument is quite versatile in that it can be used for plucking on a ballad as well as full out strumming for a heavier tune. It can also be used as either a filler instrument in the background or as the main instrument in a song. It adds a rootsy effect to any arrangement. There are a lot of good acoustic guitars on the market and you don't need to spend tons of money to get a good sounding instrument (compared to purchasing an electric guitar, which also needs an amp and pedals).

For the past decade the electric/acoustic has been quite popular. An electric/acoustic guitar has a preamp built into the body, which allows the guitar to bypass an amp and be plugged directly into a P.A. (public address system). Although this makes gigging a lot easier, you will find that in the studio most engineers still prefer to mic the guitar. No matter how good a pickup and preamp you have in your electric/acoustic, the microphones used in studios are a lot more sensitive. Sometimes an engineer will mic your guitar in one channel and use the pickup from your guitar to go into another channel. This way he can use both signals in the mix. This is a fairly common practice in the studio.

Acoustic/electrics have had periods of great popularity. They are sometimes miked in one channel and plugged directly into the board into another channel.

STUDIO TIPS FOR USING ACOUSTIC GUITARS

You may think you only need to own one acoustic guitar, but this simply isn't the case. Different acoustics have different purposes.

• 12-string acoustics are used for background and full strumming.

• Smaller-bodied guitars are good for complex musical pieces.

• Bigger bodied acoustics are great for rhythm guitar parts.

• Cutaway acoustics are good for playing higher up the neck.

When looking for a good acoustic guitar for recording, you will want different features than if you were looking to buy a guitar for live performance. Good live-performance acoustic guitars tend to have a lot more projection and bottom end. Acoustic guitars best suited for the studio will possess an overall even tone—not too strong in the low frequencies (which cause boomy tones) and not too strong in the high, piercing frequencies (which tend to stick out too much). To start, you may merely want to purchase a medium-sized acoustic with a cutaway and preamp and eventually keep adding guitars, as you get busier within the business.

Technical Tip No. 6–EQ for Acoustic Guitars

Acoustic guitars, if not properly EQed, can sound boomy. Try working between 80Hz and 220Hz to cut back on boominess.

For top end sparkle, boost your highs to between 5kHz and 10kHz.

Be careful not to go too bright or you get harsh, piercing tones, which seem to be in the upper mid-range (between 1kHz and 2kHz).

Always be sure to put on new strings before going to a session to record acoustic tracks. This pertains to all guitars, but especially acoustics. Of course, you will want them well stretched so there won't be tuning problems in the studio. New strings are what create the "crispy" sound heard in songs with acoustic guitars.

New strings also allow your acoustic guitar to be properly intonated (more on this later), which makes for a perfectly tuned guitar no matter where you are playing on the fretboard. Of all the instruments you will own, bad intonation will be most apparent on an acoustic guitar because of the many open chords that are normally played. Open chords are notorious for bringing out bad intonation.

Furthermore, if you need to re-record a part at a later time, having new strings will assure that the sound will be consistent with the previous recording.

Also be sure to carry a supply of picks that vary from soft to hard. Soft picks are great for strumming and give the guitar a percussive sound. The harder picks can be used for picking or strumming. More experienced players usually prefer harder picks because they produce a better tone. Experiment on your own and you will be able to hear the different effects the picks create.

Technical Tip No. 7—Guitar Maintenance

It's a good practice to make sure your guitar is in proper working order. If you aren't that handy with guitar repairs, you can easily find a guitar technician who can do the work for you at a reasonable price.

You'll want to make sure your neck is not warped, since that can create buzzes and dead notes throughout the fingerboard. These problems become very obvious in the studio. For an acoustic guitar, check that your pickup is distributing the sound evenly throughout the strings. If your strings are too low or too high, your action needs to be adjusted.

SUGGESTED LISTENING FOR ACOUSTIC GUITARS
Ry Cooder
Ani DiFranco
John Mayer
Joni Mitchell
Don Ross
Merle Travis

CLASSICAL GUITARS (NYLON STRINGS)

Classical guitars have nylon strings rather than the steel strings used for acoustics. Usually, nylon strings do not have balls at the end (some ball-end sets are available, but most classical guitarists use the higher quality traditional strings). The strings are threaded through holes in the bridge and then knotted. The necks on the classical guitar are shorter and wider than a steel-string acoustic. There are usually only 19 frets and the body joins the neck at the 12th fret instead of the 14th.

STUDIO TIPS FOR THE CLASSICAL GUITAR

Since the classical guitar has a shorter neck, your execution during certain passages can be limited. Usually music that is written for the classical guitar bears this in mind, but it's a good idea to have a cutaway classical just in case a nylon-string sound and higher pitches are wanted.

CHALLENGES OF CLASSICAL GUITARS

If you prefer playing guitar with your fingernails rather than a pick, you can be in for a stressful recording career. Even though the best tone comes from using your fingernails on the classical guitar, there is a lot of high maintenance that goes with it. The obvious problem is that you can damage your nails just before a session. This can easily happen just by lugging gear back and forth from the studio. But if using your nails is an important aspect of your playing, you will need to make sure you have all the right "nail gear" to protect and repair any problems.

Although most classical guitarists prefer using their nails, playing a nylon-string guitar with a pick at a session is also acceptable today. Try different picks to see which ones are more comfortable and sound the closest to using your fingernails. You can purchase leather picks, which sound the closest to real nails.

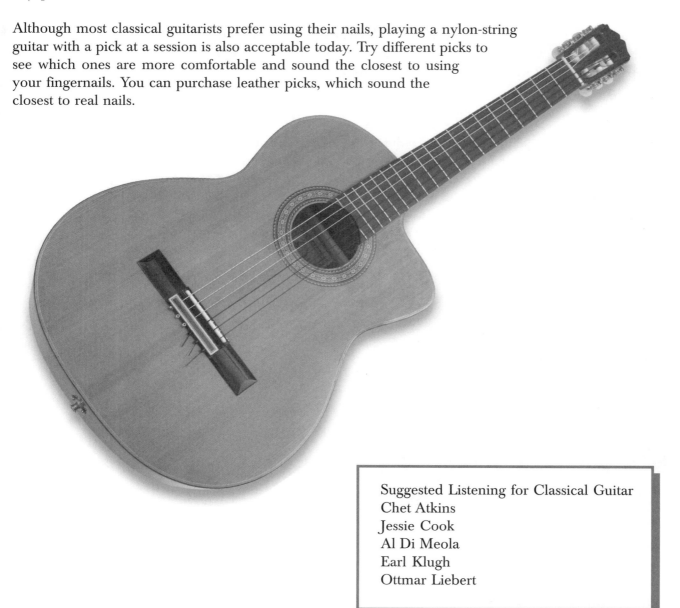

Suggested Listening for Classical Guitar
Chet Atkins
Jessie Cook
Al Di Meola
Earl Klugh
Ottmar Liebert

THE GUITAR SETUP

The importance of having your guitars set up properly cannot be overemphasized. It has a major impact on the sound and playability of any guitar. Some of this you can do yourself, such as making sure the intonation is correct, but other procedures should be done by an accomplished luthier or guitar technician. Checking the setup should be done several times a year, and it is relatively inexpensive.

Below are some things to consider when bringing your guitar into the shop. This may seem like a lot of extra work, but remember that your guitar is just like a car: the better it is tuned up, the better it will function. The last thing you want to do is arrive at a session and realize a setup problem has made your axe unplayable.

ACTION

The action is the distance (or height) from the strings to the fretboard of the guitar. When guitarists talk about the action, they are referring to the energy they need to exert with the fretting hand. A "good action" allows one to make a clear sound without applying unnecessary pressure to the strings. "Bad action" means the strings are set either too low (creating buzzes and rattles), or too high (making it difficult to play).

> **Technical Tip No. 8—Action**
>
> *If you change the gauge of your strings from light to heavy (or vice versa) you may need to adjust your action. Before bringing your guitar in for a setup, make sure that you are happy with the guage of your strings.*

Make sure that whoever is repairing your instrument is clear on what you are trying to accomplish with your action. Generally, the higher the action, the better the tone of your guitar—but keep in mind that it will also be more difficult to play.

THE NUT

The nut is the thin strip of material that sits between the fretboard and the head. Usually it is constructed of graphite, bone or metal. Although many musicians are concerned about the type of nut installed on the guitar, the most frequently underestimated problem is that it may not be cut properly. An improperly cut nut will not allow the strings to vibrate as well as they should, which in turn affects the tone. Be sure to ask your guitar tech to check the quality of the nut. Sometimes simply filing it will bring positive results, or it may need to be replaced if the original one is of poor quality or has been damaged.

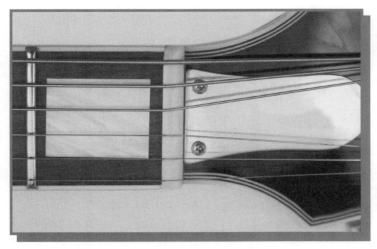

Acoustic and electrics use the same types of nuts. They are constructed either from bone, graphite or metal (for better sustain).

NECK ADJUSTMENTS

Often, "bad action" can be a direct result of a warped neck. Neck warpage can happen if your guitar is exposed to extreme temperatures, improper care or rough treatment from traveling—especially by plane. Sometimes, all that is required is a simple adjustment of the truss rod, which runs through the length of the neck and is used to adjust the amount of bow. It is tricky because every guitar must have a certain amount of bow to work properly—but not too much or too little. If the neck has sustained serious damage it may have to be repaired. Checking the bow in the neck is a standard part of a guitar setup.

STRINGS

For every guitar you own, you will need the appropriate strings. For the most part, classical guitars use nylon strings, acoustic guitars use bronze or brass strings and electric guitars use nickel or stainless-steel strings. As far as tone is concerned, heavier gauge strings are a better choice (but are more difficult to play). Lighter gauges are thinner sounding, but are a lot easier to play and bend notes with. You'll have to experiment to see which strings are most comfortable for you.

INTONATION

One thing that becomes crystal clear during a studio session is the importance of a perfectly tuned guitar. Tuning problems become very apparent once you have laid down your guitar tracks, especially when playing with electronic keyboards, since they are usually always in perfect tune. Even after using a tuner, your guitar may still be out of tune in certain areas of the fretboard. If you have already installed new strings and are still having trouble getting in tune, another factor to consider is the guitar's intonation.

Correct intonation means that all the strings on your guitar are the proper distance from inside of the nut to where they first touch the *saddle* (elevates the strings at or just before the bridge). This distance is called the scale length and is the part of the string that vibrates to create a pitch. The scale length must be totally accurate for the strings to be consistently in tune throughout the fretboard. If you play an open C chord on the 1st fret and then play a barred C chord further up the fretboard and one of them is out of tune, it is because the intonation is off. You will need to either increase or decrease the scale length with adjustments made at the saddle.

CORRECTING YOUR INTONATION

Most electric guitars have adjustable saddles. This means that the scale length of each string intonation can be adjusted to correct intonation problems.

The following steps are for guitars that have adjustable bridges. In order to correct your intonation you will need a flat head screwdriver and an electronic guitar tuner.

1. Using your tuner, play the open 1st string (high E string) and notice where it reads on the tuner.

2. Play the string again, this time fretting it at the 12th fret. If the note at the 12th fret is flat (or lower in pitch than your open 1st string), you will have to adjust your saddle forward moving it closer to your pickups. This shortens the scale length of your string. Then adjust your saddle by using a screwdriver that fits into the screws of your saddle (see photo page 22).

3. If the note at the 12th fret is higher in pitch than your open string, you will need to lengthen your string, which means moving the saddle away from the pickups.

4. Keep repeating this process until the open string and the fretted string read exactly the same pitch on the tuner.

5. Check and adjust the remaining strings by repeating steps 1 through 4.

OTHER TYPES OF BRIDGES

Fixed bridges, found on steel-string acoustic and classical guitars, are glued directly on to the soundboard and cannot move. If you have intonation problems on your acoustic guitar, it is more than likely caused by a warped neck. If the neck has recently been adjusted and your action is correct, there may be a fault in the saddle or frets, which would have to be fixed by a guitar technician.

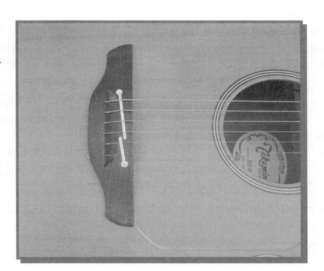

Floating bridges are generally found on arch top hollow body electric guitars. This type of bridge is not glued to the soundboard; the tension of the strings keeps it stationary. A floating bridge can be moved backward or forward to correct intonation. Some of the more modern floating bridges also have individual screws for further fine tuning.

THE STUDIO GUITARIST'S TOOLBOX

To be properly prepared for any situation that can arise in the studio, you will need to create a toolbox. Your toolbox will consist of accessories as well as a few tools necessary for quick emergency repairs.

ACCESSORIES

TUNER

Most guitarists own an electronic tuner, since it is an invaluable tool for performing live and practicing, as well as playing in the studio. You should check your tuning frequently when you are on a session. There will often be other musicians involved, and being able to use a tuner without having to actually hear the guitar is courteous to everyone around you. At the same time, because of budget considerations, no one wants to wait around a long time while you take the time to tune by ear. Making a tuning pedal part of your foot pedal rig when playing electric guitar is a good idea. It is customary to use a small, handheld tuner when playing acoustic guitar, or when you are not using your foot pedals.

CAPO

Capos are great gadgets that are placed around the neck to raise the pitch of the strings. They allow you to transpose (change the key) of a chord progression but still use the same chord shapes. They are excellent for songs that require an open chord effect. Let's say you are playing a progression with A–E–D in open chords. The vocalist realizes that the key is too low and wants to transpose it up a whole tone to B–F#–E. You would have to play the first two chords as barre chords, which would change the sound of the song. Instead, you can put your capo on your 2nd fret and play the same open chord shapes. Your fingerings would still look like A–E–D, but they would sound like B–F#–E.

You can also experiment with using your capo higher up the fretboard to get an almost mandolin or 12-string-guitar sound. This can be a nice, additional sound to use over another recorded guitar track to brighten or thicken it. The other great thing about capos is that you can still use the open-string licks you play with open chords, which are difficult if not impossible with barred chords.

Technical Tip No. 11—Capos

When purchasing a capo, keep in mind that if your guitar has a flat fretboard, you will need a capo that has a flat bar. If your guitar has a more rounded fretboard, the capo bar will need to be rounded.

STRINGS AND STRING WINDERS

Since you never know when or how many times during a session you will break a string, make sure that you pack three or four extras for each string. And don't forget your handy string winder, which not only saves time but has a groove built into it that allows you to quickly pull out saddle pegs on acoustic guitars.

SLIDES

Most session players have some knowledge of how to play with a slide. Slides are made from either glass or metal and fit around a finger. They create the gliding sound so commonly used in blues and country music. Each material produces a different sound. It's best to have a specific guitar set aside for slide playing since they sound the best with a guitar that has a very high action. Normally, slide guitar players use open tunings and place their slide on the 3rd or 4th finger.

EMERGENCY REPAIR TOOLS

Cables and soldering gun. Have a few cables (short and long), a soldering gun and paste to do any cable repairs or other amp/guitar repairs as needed. Be sure to purchase high quality cables, since they make a difference in your tone and don't break down as easily.

Batteries, adapters, power strip and D.I. boxes. If your acoustic guitars have a preamp you should have a few extra batteries. Also keep extra batteries for your handheld tuner or pedals. If your effects use AC adapters be sure to have an extra working one ready just in case. A power strip (or power bar) is useful for plugging in your amp and adapters. Be sure to get one with a long cord in case you are positioned in an awkward spot in the recording room. A D.I. (direct input) box with a ground switch can also be helpful if ground problems occur.

Fuses, tubes and flashlight. For tube amps, you will need to have extra tubes and fuses. Keep both of these wrapped up in some sort of cloth to protect them from breaking. A flashlight may be necessary to help you see inside your amp during repairs.

Screwdrivers, needle nose pliers and pocket knife. These will come in handy for many miscellaneous repairs, such as fixing pedals or raising the poles on your pickups.

Pen, paper and business cards. You should have something to write on for any notes you want to take during a session. And don't forget, the studio is a great place to network with other musicians, so be sure to have plenty of business cards on hand.

For more information about setting up and caring for your guitar, check out *Guitar Shop: Setup and Maintenance* by John Carruthers (Alfred/National Guitar Workshop, #18479).

CHAPTER 2
THE AMPLIFIER

During the swing era (the 1930s), it was difficult to hear the guitarist above the horn section and the vocalist. This resulted in the invention of the electric guitar and amplifier. The amplifier is often an ignored component in the guitar chain. Understanding how your amplifier works is fundamental to creating a great tone in the studio as well as in live performances. Your amplification is a vital link to getting a great tone and guitarists often spend years in search of that magical sound.

TUBE VS. SOLID STATE AMPS

The first amps to come on the scene were made using tubes. They were of basic design, consisting of vacuum tubes, basic circuitry and speakers. Today, tube amps pretty much have the same components. They continue to be the favored amp of many guitarists because of their warm tone, great dynamic capabilities and ability to distort.

In the mid 1960s, solid-state amps (also called "trannies" because they used transistors instead of tubes) were introduced on the market and declared to be the answer to the modern guitarist's amplification needs. They cost a lot less, they were very clean sounding and needed less maintenance. Unfortunately, the most important aspect of the amp for many was missing: a warm tone. Luckily, a lot has been done over the years to improve the sound of the solid-state amps, which now outsell tube amps. Solid-state amps are quite popular amongst jazz and country players, who primarily require a very clean tone.

Hybrid amplifiers are a combination of tube and solid-state technology. They take the best from both, using a tube preamp, and solid state power amp or vice versa. Manufacturers then market the amp at a lower cost than an all tube amp. Marshall, Peavey and Fender are some of the companies that were offering hybrid amplifiers at the time of this writing.

Your goal with using any amp that you own is to know how to create a good tone. Being knowledgeable of the different configurations of amps is also essential, as well as being able to manipulate sounds requested during a session.

STAGES OF AN AMPLIFIER

In order to better understand how an amplifier functions (and how to handle it in a studio setting), we first need to take a look at how the signal is affected as it goes though the different stages of the circuitry.

When the signal from your guitar enters your amplifier, it passes through several gain stages before it arrives at its final destination: the speaker. Each stage has a different function in making the signal ready to be used in the next chain of the circuitry.

THE POWER SUPPLY

The AC current generated from your wall outlet is broken down and veered to separate parts of your amp according to its demands. Some of the electricity goes to the power tubes and some to the preamp tubes. The quality of your amp's power supply directly affects every stage that comes after it. Excellent circuitry throughout the rest of the chain will not compensate for a poor quality power supply.

THE PREAMP

This is the first stage of the signal. Since the signal emanating from the guitar is quite weak, a fixed voltage is attached to it, which prepares it to be increased. This section of the chain is where you will find your tone controls, effects loop and reverb. The preamp is also where the tone of your amp is formed.

THE POWER AMP

The next stage in the chain of the circuitry is the power amp. Here, the weak signal is transformed by being boosted. The more superior your power amp, the less likely it is to alter or color the tone as it is being augmented. As with the power supply, the quality of your power amp dictates how good your tone will be in the end.

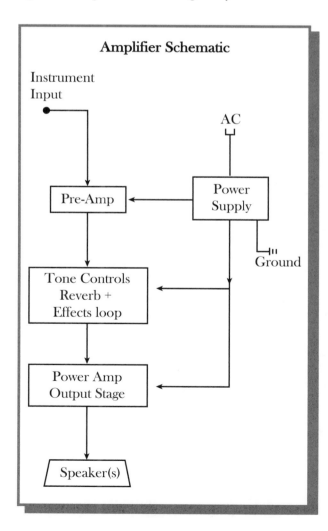

AMPLIFIER CONFIGURATIONS

There are three possible amplifier configurations:

    Combo

    Head and cabinet

    Rackmount and cabinet

Each configuration has its own characteristics, and professional guitarists (session as well as many live players) tend to collect all of them. Experienced producers are familiar with the different configurations and the particular sounds they create, therefore you should be prepared to know them as well.

When considering amplifiers, ask yourself what you are actually trying to accomplish with the amp. It all boils down to two main factors: either you are looking for a clean amp to provide a sparkling, crisp signal (such as a Fender or Vox) or you are looking for a dirty amp, which gives you guts and great distortion (like a Marshall or Mesa Boogie). There are many first-rate amps being manufactured today, but Fender and Marshall make the foundational amps that most others have been built upon. It is therefore advantageous that you get acquainted with what both of them have to offer.

COMBO

Some combo amplifiers have great tones (especially the vintage or reissue amps). Unfortunately they are not as versatile as rackmounts or heads.

Combo amps are the easiest type of amp to lug around to sessions, but they are not as versatile as the others. You can get some excellent tones from your combo, and often it's all that is needed. Many combo amps have an open back, which lets the speaker sound escape through the back as well as the front. Because of that, placing a mic on either side in the studio will get fairly good results. A Fender Deluxe is an example of a combo amp used by many great players, including Steve Gibson, who is one of the top guns in the Nashville recording scene. Also, the legendary Albert King played his '67 Gibson Flying V through a Peavey Special 212 Combo to get his signature blues tone.

HEAD AND CABINETS

*You can mix and match your
head and cabinets.*

Amp heads allow you to plug into various types of cabinets to generate a variety of sounds. You can also try putting different heads through one cabinet. It takes some experimentation, but mixing and matching heads and cabinets is a common practice amongst guitarists. Most cabinets have closed backs, which forces all the sound to go to the front, creating a punchier tone with a lot of low-end drive. Marshall heads and cabinets have been used for years by the likes of Jeff Beck, Ace Frehley of Kiss and Eric Johnson.

Technical Tip No. 12—Natural Distortion

If you are looking for great natural distortion (strictly from the amp), you will need to experiment with different amps. Try playing a guitar with humbucker pickups through a 50-watt combo amp. If the amp is over 50 watts, it will sound pretty clean, but the smaller amps tend to allow the pickup's full capacity to come through. You will find that the smaller the amp, the more natural the distortion will sound.

RACKMOUNT AND CABINET

This combination gives you the most flexibility and is quite useful during a recording session since it allows you to have many sounds at your disposal. A rackmount amp lets you alter the signal at each step as it moves through the chain of the circuitry.

There are many variations of rackmounts, but they mostly consist of:
    Preamp
    Multi-effects unit
    Power amp

If you wanted to, you could even use the pre-amp of your head and then plug directly into the effects unit of the rackmount, then into a cabinet of your choice. The possibilities are limitless. Wes Borland (formerly of Limp Bizkit) uses rackmounts. His gear consists of a Mesa Boogie head going into a rackmount then into a Mesa Boogie speaker cabinet.

Rackmounts are great for the studio since they provide many sounds from which to choose.

MODELING AMPLIFIERS

Also pegged as "smart amps," modeling amplifiers are digital amplifiers that have a wide compilation of vintage amp sounds. The tones these amps are attempting to reproduce run the gamut from Fender Tweeds to Mesa Boogies. The great thing about this new trend is you have a wide range of sounds at your disposal for a lot less money than buying each amp individually. The downside is the sounds are not perfect replications of the original sounds they attempt to emulate. But they do come pretty close.

Modeling amps reproduce fairly good vintage and modern tones.

Although the concept of modeling technology (DSP or digital signal processing) has been with us since the 1970s, Roland was the first to introduce the technology to the guitar world. Yamaha and Rocktron also came up with their own version of what is called COSM (composite object sound modeling). These amps have aimed at reproducing all the nuances and dynamic ranges of the traditional amplifiers (which means you can play hard on your guitar and the sound will actually distort).

Luckily for session players, modeling amps perform best in a recording environment in which you are going direct (not using microphones). At this writing, the Line 6 Flextone II Series is a very popular choice for guitarists delving into the digital phenomenon.

In the same manner that hybrids were designed to combine tube and solid-state technology, modular hybrids combine digital and analog technology. An example of this is Fender's Cyber Twin. Since the manufacturers feel that modeling technology has not yet been perfected, they have united both schools of thought to create a product that has more realistic vintage sounds.

AMP MAINTENANCE

An amp is similar to a guitar in that they both need to be maintained fairly regularly (especially any amp with tube technology). Amplifiers take a lot more abuse than guitars do and you need to stay on top of it to guarantee they are operating correctly.

Most musicians are aware of the dangers associated with the high voltages that run through their tube amps, but remember, your transistor amp can store enough power in its power supply to kill you. With that said, unless you are really comfortable with your electronic skills, it is best to get a qualified repairperson to do any needed repairs to your amp. If you do want to go ahead and do your own repairs, you will need to proceed with great caution.

TUBES

With the exception of tube amplifiers, tubes (also called valves or vacuum tubes) have all but disappeared from the maze of today's advancing technology. Tubes are chiefly made from glass, and even though they have been improved from their original design, they remain quite fragile. They can easily be damaged by extreme temperature changes or being bumped around while on gigs. This, combined with the loud volumes at which amps are played, makes it important to change the tubes regularly. Tubes can also become microphonic, which means that the pieces inside the tube break off and make it act like a microphone, picking up all sorts of buzzes and rattles.

Since tubes are made from glass, they need to be treated with special care. If your tubes seem frosty or have a bluish hue, you should change them fairly soon.

Following are some pointers to help you keep your tubes in good working order:

1. Always turn your power switch on and wait a minute or so before turning on your Standby. This gives your tubes a chance to warm up rather than shocking them into starting.

2. Be sure to keep your amp well ventilated and clean. Since tubes get fairly hot, any buildup of dust can effectively keep its internal cooling system from working its best.

3. If you're poking around the tubes in order to check them, be sure to use wooden chopsticks. Turn off your amp beforehand if your hand is actually going to be near the tubes or close to anything that can conduct current. Your amp can store power for several days, so you must be very careful.

4. Immediately upon hearing crackling, buzzes or popping, change the appropriate tubes before they cause any damage to the amp.

Technical Tip No. 13—Changing Tubes

As much as possible, try and match the tubes you are replacing with similar tubes from the same company or the same quality. Because tubes are made by hand, there will always be variances from tube to tube (even within the same company), but you stand a better chance of getting a match if you stick to the same brand.

Be sure to purchase superior tubes, as they will have a great impact on your sound.

SPEAKERS

The last thing you want to discover in the studio is a blown speaker. Obviously, it is not practical to carry an extra speaker in your toolbox, so check it regularly to make sure it is in good working order.

If you've blown a speaker, it's important to know the reason so the problem will not recur. Some guitarists have been known to play a bass through their guitar amp. If you are doing that because you don't have a bass amp, or simply for convenience sake, just be sure not to push the amp too hard. You may blow a speaker if you push your speaker too much. Speakers can also blow just from regular wear and tear. Since the cones are made from paper, they can easily get wet or dry out from overexposure to sunlight.

Upgrading the speaker(s) in your amp is suggested if you aren't happy with the tone, or would like to attempt getting a different sound. To avoid problems, replace it with a speaker that is somewhat similar in its electrical configurations to the original. At this writing, Celestion and Jensen make popular speakers used for replacement. If you are looking for a bluesy, rootsy sound, you may want to experiment with speakers that have alnico magnets (made from a combination of several metals), which tend to distort at a lower volume. For a cleaner sound, try speakers with ceramic magnets (good for jazz and country). A general rule to remember is the bigger the magnet, the more power it can handle, which results in a cleaner tone.

> ### Technical Tip No. 14—Troubleshooting Your Speaker
> *If there is no sound from your amplifier, first make sure that your speaker was not accidentally unplugged. If that is not the problem, you can try placing a nine-volt battery across the terminals of the speaker. There should be some kind of popping sound. If not, you will need new speakers.*

FUSES

Fuses are essentially electric safety valves protecting your amp from possible hazards. They will blow when a tube is trying to absorb too much power. If the fuse wasn't a part of the amp circuitry, many things could fry, including you. Always read and follow the fuse values. If you don't have or can't find the same value that is presently in your amp, temporarily purchase a smaller value. You should never use a fuse that is larger than what is endorsed by the amp manufacturer.

CHAPTER 3
GUITAR EFFECTS FOR THE STUDIO

When it comes to guitar accessories, there seems to be no end to what is available, particularly in the digital domain. As far as effects for the studio go, it's common to own a broad collection of effects, but you don't need to break the bank trying to purchase everything. In this chapter we will discuss what you will need in the studio to cover the most territory.

Guitar effects are either analog (stomp boxes) or digital multi-effects units (floor or rackmounts). Analog stomp boxes have only one effect per unit and are a lot more visual and straight forward in their application, whereas a digital multi-effects unit has several sounds contained in one unit. Multi-effect units normally contain different banks, which let you access its various preset sounds. You can also purchase units that combine analog technology with digital (such as preamps).

You can purchase fairly inexpensive individual stomp boxes to meet your effects needs.

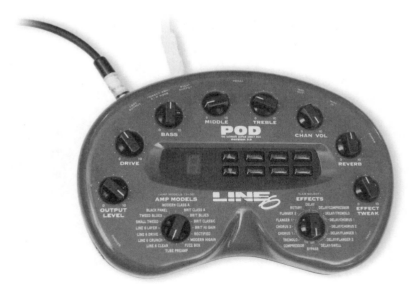

*Digital multi-effects units have come a long way in producing a fairly
authentic simulation of the original stomp boxes and amp sounds.*

If you're shopping around for effects, try doing the same thing discussed in Chapter 1 with regard to guitars. Simply go to your local music store and try some of their effects. The best situation is to plug into a guitar and amp similar to your own so you have a good idea of the sound you'll get if you decide to purchase. And don't forget to ask your friends to try out or swap effects.

All guitar effects are broken down into three different categories:

1. Signal enhancers—Compressors, distortions, wah-wah pedals and EQ

2. Ambient effects—Reverb and delays

3. Time-based effects—Pitch shifters, chorus, flangers and delay (since delays also effect time, they also fit into this category)

SIGNAL ENHANCERS

As the name implies, these effects enhance or embellish your signal rather than alter it (with the exception of raising the gain).

COMPRESSORS

This effect acts as a sort of volume pedal in that it will stabilize the volume as it goes to the amplifier to a pre-set level, regardless of the dynamics you play on your guitar. In other words, it evens out the highs and lows of the volume that it receives.

One advantage of using compression is that it automatically adds sustain to your sound (which is sometimes the only reason guitarists use it). The disadvantage of too much compression is that it can significantly limit your dynamics, specifically in the high end. Using your EQ can solve some of this. Be sure to set your compression to a level that still allows the expressiveness of your playing to shine through.

> **Technical Tip No. 15—Combining Compression**
>
> *Compressors can also make your other effects sound much more vibrant. Try using your compression to see how it affects your delays. Using this effect lets you achieve amazing feedback without distortion.*
>
> *If you have a stomp box compressor, be sure to by-pass it when not playing, since it will raise the noise signal that is coming from the rest of your effects.*

DISTORTIONS

The sound of overdriven tube amplifiers has always been one of the most desirous elements of the rock guitar sound. Unfortunately, a distorted sound is not appropriate for every style of music you may be called upon to play at a session. Having a separate unit for distortion, rather than obtaining it through an amp, gives the guitarist more control.

The early distortion stomp boxes didn't really sound like overdriven amps. They sounded a lot fuzzier and were appropriately dubbed fuzztones. Jimi Hendrix, as well as Jeff Beck (while with the Yardbirds), frequently used a fuzztone. Although vintage sounds from the 1960s are commonly sought after, most guitarists desire an overdriven tube amp simulation.

Modern technology has made it quite easy to duplicate great distortion. Digital units have a myriad of vintage-to-modern sounds from which to choose, which is very practical in a studio environment. Be aware that different guitars get different results when distortion is applied. A single-coil pickup, which is fairly thin sounding, may call for a different distortion than your double-coil pickup, which naturally has a meatier sound. Also, your double-coil pickup going through distortion may really rock, but can easily get lost in the mix once it's put in with all the other instruments. Record yourself while jamming or playing live to see how well your solos and rhythm parts stand out.

> ### Technical Tip No. 16—Using Distortion
>
> *You should never use distortion to hide bad technique or cover up bad tone. Too much distortion can make your sound too far back in the mix. Excessive distortion will muddy a quick passage of music, leaving no distinction between the notes.*
>
> *If you are trying to correct a thin sound, instead of drowning it with distortion, try using EQ as well as sustain. Always work on first having a great tone before applying distortion. This also pertains to using all other effects.*

WAH-WAH PEDALS

You may only infrequently use a wah-wah pedal for recording, but this is one accessory you can't do without. Either a stomp box version or as a part of a multi-effects foot pedal, this effect will find its voice in a variety of styles, from funky tunes to rock. But don't be fooled by its straight-ahead application. You will still need to spend some time getting a good rhythm with your foot to produce convincing results. It does take a little bit of practice but it is well worth the effort. Listen to artists such as Jimi Hendrix or Steve Vai to hear some great wah-wah playing. One problem with wah-wah pedals is the internal mechanisms tend to wear down quickly. There are more modern versions (such as those by Morley) that use optical technology to turn the unit on and off, thus reducing the wear and tear of the components.

EQ

Equalization (EQ) is the method of manipulating precise frequencies from your instrument. There are two types of EQs used to do this:

- Graphic EQ–used to affect your overall sound

- Parametric EQ–Applied to very specific or single frequencies.

> ### Technical Tip No. 17—Working with EQ
>
> *You can use your EQ as a booster for your signal (for example, for soloing). Make sure you set it up so that it increases the volume without changing your tone (unless that is what you want).*

For example, you can use a graphic EQ to warm up some of your tone by manipulating your mid-range, or accentuate a specific frequency in the high-end with a parametric EQ, allowing your solos to cut through a little better.

AMBIENT EFFECTS

In recording, ambience is the name given for the overall echo that is detected in any given room. It is the result of sound waves that reflect off, or are absorbed by, the surfaces present. Ambient effects endeavor to reproduce these naturally occurring sound waves.

REVERB

Spring reverb, found in most amplifiers, was one of the first reverbs developed. It works by sending the signal through a spring. The amount of time taken to travel to the end of the spring creates delay.

Although spring reverbs coming from a tube amplifier have in the past been the most desirous, digital reverbs offer great results as well. Digital reverbs can simulate practically any ambience needed in the studio, ranging from that of a small jazz club to a huge cathedral.

> ### Technical Tip No. 18—Using Reverb
>
> *Many sounds coming from a multi-effects unit have a preset reverb already configured into their parameters. You will therefore need to keep your amplifier's reverb down to a minimum to maintain clarity in your playing.*

DELAYS

It is important to distinguish between reverb that is a naturally occurring echo, and delay, which is an artificially produced separate repetition of an original sound. Although delay can create the effect of spaciousness, it can also be manipulated to have a "slap" echo. This slap, which was popularized in early rockabilly recordings, is still a commonly-used effect.

ANALOG VS DIGITAL DELAY

Analog delay was first designed to emulate tape delay (which was physically quite bulky and required frequent demagnetization of the tape heads). By using transistor technology, analog delays replaced tape heads with IC chips (integrated circuits). These units were much smaller but generated too much noise at about half a second of delay. Digital delays, which use digital code to handle the signal, allow for less distortion and longer delay.

TIME EFFECTS

Time effects distort the original signal by first sampling (making a digital copy of it) then delaying it in time, and then blending it back with the original signal.

CHORUS

Chorus units were used extensively in the 1970s on almost every pop song. They imitate a sort of 12-string-guitar or multi-guitar effect, adding fullness and richness to the original sound. Artists who used chorus extensively include Andy Summers of The Police and, more recently, Kurt Cobain of Nirvana.

> ### Technical Tip No. 19—Chorus
>
> *For a natural chorus effect on your acoustic guitar, use a 12-string and slightly detune the unisons of the double strings. This variation in the pitch, and the fact that you are not hitting all the strings exactly at the same time as you strum (producing a small delay) creates a chorus effect.*

PITCH SHIFTERS (HARMONIZERS)

A pitch shifter alters the tuning of the sampled signal. The range of the detuning can be anywhere from a subtle chorus effect all the way to intervals of 5ths (which is why it is sometimes called a harmonizer). The newer pitch shifters are able to adjust to the key in which you are playing, allowing you to harmonize with yourself diatonically (using only notes found in the key). Often, what sounds like a double lead guitar solo is actually someone using this effect.

FLANGERS

Although a flanger is considered a vintage sound, you will find it in many multi-effects units. It produces a "whooshing" sound. A popular technique is to combine flanging with chorus. Analog flangers (and choruses) generally have a warmer sound but they are not as clean and accurate as their digital counterparts. For an example of a flanger listen to the Edge on U2's song, "New Year's Day."

DELAY

On page 37, we discussed delay as an ambient effect, but it also doubles as a time effect since it manipulates the signal by repeating it. The delay time can be varied to fit the desired result. For example, Steve Vai used 30% delay for the tune "Skyscraper," while on "Blue Powder," he had his delay set at 60%.

> ### Technical Tip No. 20—Effects in the Studio
>
> *When bringing effects into the studio, be sure to communicate what you are thinking of using with the engineer, who may be planning to use the same effects on the mixing console.*

THE SIGNAL CHAIN

Even though multi-effects units have all the effects preset in their proper order, you need to have a good grasp on the order in which your effects are set up, especially if you use pedals or are trying to change the sequence in your multi-effects unit to achieve different results.

In the box below you will see an illustration of the effects chain in its proper sequence. You may not use all these effects at once, but this gives you a general idea of how they should be placed. Most multi-effects units allow you to change the sequence of the chain.

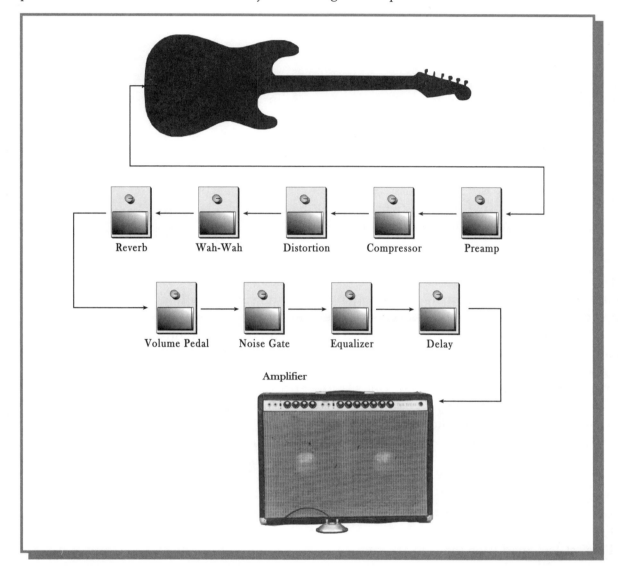

If you are hoping to divide your effects between before (pre) and after (post) the preamp, but still before the power amp, the rule of thumb is this: place signal conditioners before the preamp, put time effects and others after the preamp. If you desire to experiment with different ordering, viewing your effects as belonging to the three categories discussed here will help.

A CAUTION ABOUT EFFECTS

It goes without saying that effects are necessary tools for the modern session player, but what you should always keep in the forefront is tastefulness and appropriateness to the style of music you are playing. Educate yourself about what type of effects are used for certain styles of music and try to emulate great artists who use these effects. Many guitar magazines and books not only reveal the guitars and amps that certain artists play, but also the effects that are used on different songs. Check out, for example, *Guitar Shop: Getting Your Sound*, by Tobias Hurwitz (Alfred/National Guitar Workshop, #18424).

PART 2—A PRO IN THE STUDIO
CHAPTER 4
ATTITUDE, STYLES AND CHORDS

In this chapter we will cover some essentials for success in the studio, such as attitude, knowledge of different styles of music, improvisation and chart reading skills.

ATTITUDE IN THE STUDIO—THE SIX B'S

1. **BE READY**

   Before you arrive to the studio, you should make sure all your equipment is in tip-top shape. The strings on each of the guitars that you are bringing with you should be fairly new. If you have just put on a brand new pair of strings, make sure to stretch them well so they will not go out of tune too quickly while you are recording. You will need to be clear on what equipment the producer (or the person hiring you) is expecting you to bring. Find out if they are looking for a specific electric guitar sound, or if it is acoustic tracks that you will be recording. If they are not specific about gear, find out what style of music will be involved and gauge what to bring based on that information.

2. **BE PUNCTUAL**

   If you think it's the cool musician thing to be fashionably late, think again. Studios charge by the hour and if you are 15 minutes late for a session, you will have used up a quarter of an hour. It would not be appreciated by the artist who is paying you to be there, and the producer would think twice about hiring you again. If you are going to a location you have never been to before, get proper directions and the phone number of the studio in case you get lost or are delayed due to traffic problems. Leave yourself plenty of extra time for travel and set up. Also, ask if there is parking close to the studio. Sometimes studios are located down hidden alleys or in industrial plazas and are hard to find.

3. **BE PROFESSIONAL**

   Having a great attitude is an essential trait to have for a successful career. There are a lot of phenomenal musicians out there, and your abilities added to a professional attitude will help set you apart from the competition.

   If you plan to be considered professional in this business, you must own a cell phone. Studio owners get frustrated if you are late (even if it's not your fault) and it is just plain courtesy to let them know you are running behind schedule. This allows the time spent waiting for you to be used constructively. Cell phones also give you the ability to check your answering machine or voice mail at home while away, so you won't miss important opportunities. You can leave your cell phone number on your out going message so you can always be reached. Studios call their list of musicians to see who's available and, if you miss the call, someone else may get the gig. That gig could be the very one that will establish you and get you in the loop. If you want to be taken seriously, it is a good idea to call in several times a day while away and return your calls immediately.

Another tool that is quite beneficial is posting your own Website with gigs you are playing, a list of your accomplishments and a contact link for people to e-mail you. Websites are quickly becoming the norm in the industry and it demonstrates to people that you are professional.

4. BE AVAILABLE

Often, sessions can last a lot longer than anticipated. If you are gigging later on that evening, you need to make sure that you have contingency plans in case the recording goes overtime. It doesn't hurt to mention any time restraints to the producer. Another option is to have a sub (substitute) on standby who you can call to stand-in for you at the gig or complete the session if it becomes necessary.

To guarantee a successful schedule, be sure you have left yourself plenty of time to get to your next destination without feeling rushed or under pressure. There is already enough pressure in the studio without adding anxiety over time issues.

5. BE FLEXIBLE

The studio setting is made up of a group of professional people working together for the attainment of one goal—serving the music. Your ideas and expertise are only a piece of the whole. Being a team player and remaining flexible and able to take directions well is very important. You may lay down a track and feel it was a great take only to find out that the producer wants to change it or try a different approach. Just remember you are being hired to bring your expertise to the table but you need to leave your ego at home.

6. BE ALERT

If you only got two hours of sleep the night before because you had a gig out of town or were up late partying, chances are it's going to show in the session. Remember that whatever is recorded is permanent and will reflect your playing, so you'll want to be performing your best at all times. Not only can sleep deprivation affect your performance, but also improper diet can cause you to be sluggish and create brain fog. If you know that lack of food affects you, bring your own lunch or some kind of energy bar so you won't feel like taking a nap when it's your turn to record.

STYLES OF MUSIC

One of the essentials of being in demand as a studio musician is versatility—being able to play in many different styles. The chart below will enable you to analyze the different characteristics of most popular styles. You don't need to learn all of these styles, but think of those in bold type as "mandatory." Naturally, you will gravitate to (and perhaps end up specializing in) those styles with which you are most comfortable. Although the chart is not comprehensive, it gives you an idea of the music you may be called upon to record. You can create a chart to analyze the different characteristics of each style for your own study. Begin by learning those that you are the most familiar with and build from there. You need to be convincing in whichever genre you are asked to play, so be sure to spend lots of time listening to musicians who play each style proficiently.

STYLE	RHYTHM For Right-Hand Picking or Strumming	STYLE VARIATIONS	COMMON SCALES	CHORDS AND PROGRESSIONS
Rock		1950s & '60s Rock **1970s Rock** Progressive Rock Heavy Metal **Alternative**	Major and Minor Pentatonic Dorian Mode Blues	Barre Power Open I–IV–V Progressions
Reggae			Major and Minor Pentatonic Dorian Mode	Barre Open I–IV–V Progressions
Country		Bluegrass Country Western Western Swing **New Country**	Major and Minor Pentatonic Major (Ionian Mode)	Barre Open I–IV–V Progressions
Blues		**Texas** Delta Urban **Rock** **Funk** Jazz Country	Major and Minor Pentatonic Mixolydian Mode Blues	Barre, Open and Extended I–IV–V, 12-Bar and its variations Turnarounds Intros Endings
Jazz		**Swing** **Latin Jazz** Fusion Smooth Bebop Free Modern	All modes of the major scale Jazz minor (melodic minor) Altered Diminished Whole-Tone Bebop	Mostly 7th Chords with Extensions ii–V–I I–vi–ii–V Cycle of 5th Progressions
Soul and Funk		Motown Old School	Major and Minor Pentatonic Mixolydian Mode Dorian Mode	Barres Extended I–IV–V and One- and Two-Chord Vamps
Latin		Afro-Cuban Beguine Tango Cha-Cha **Merengue** Montuno **Samba**	Major and Minor Harmonic Minor Exotic	Open Barre I–IV–V Progressions
Folk		**Ballads**	Major and Minor Open and Fretted Major and Minor Pentatonic	Open Barre I–IV–V Progressions

Take time to learn the rhythms that are common to the style you have to play, and analyze the main components that make it unique. For example, if you want to play blues, you could listen to such guitar greats as Stevie Ray Vaughan or Buddy Guy. Go to the appropriate jam sessions in your area and get to know the musicians. When approached in a friendly manner, most people enjoy sharing their knowledge and expertise with someone who is trying to break into the business.

This chart will deal with techniques, artists, resources and guitars appropriate to each style.

STYLE	RIGHT- AND LEFT-HAND TECHNIQUES		ARTISTS/BANDS	BOOKS AND RESOURCES	GUITARS
Rock	Strumming (pick) Chunky Downstrokes Bends Slides	Hammer-ons Pull-offs Harmonics	Eric Clapton Jimi Hendrix Lenny Kravitz Metallica Carlos Santana Steve Vai	*Mastering Rock Guitar* (Erik Halbig) (Alfred/NGW #14096)	Electric Guitars with single- and/or double-coil pickups
Reggae	Short, percussive down or upstrokes with pick		Bob Marley The Police UB40		Electric Guitar usually with single-coil pickups
Country	Strumming with pick Fingerstyle Slide Chicken Pickin' Picking with thumbpick		Albert Lee Hank Garland Jerry Reed		Electric Guitar, single-coil pickups Acoustic steel-string Dobro
Blues	Strumming with pick Fingerstyle Slide Bends Slides Hammer-on Pull-offs	Harmonics Vibrato	Kenny Burrell Robben Ford John Lee Hooker B.B. King Bonnie Raitt Stevie Ray Vaughan Muddy Waters	*Mastering Blues Guitar*, Wayne Riker (Alfred/NGW #8234)	Electric Guitar, single- or double-coil Acoustic steel-string Slide
Jazz	Comping using pick and/or fingers Fingerstyle Arpeggios Harmonics		Chet Atkins Larry Coryell Jim Hall Joe Pass Wes Montgomery Emily Remler	*The Complete Jazz Guitar Method*, Jody Fisher (Alfred/NGW #14123, 14129, 14126)	Archtop Hollow body Semi-hollow body
Soul and Funk	Short, percussive down or upstrokes with pick		James Brown Earth, Wind & Fire Kool & The Gang Parliament	*Stand Alone Funk* (Alfred/NGW #4473) *Stand Alone R&B* (Alfred/NGW#14832)	Electric Guitar usually with single-coil pickups
Latin	Fingerstyle		Jesse Cook Gypsy Kings Oscar Lopez Carlos Rubio	*Guitar Atlas: Brazil* Billy Newman (Alfred/NGW #20453)	Classical or Flamenco
Folk	Strumming with pick Fingerstyle		Ry Cooder Ani DiFranco Joni Mitchell Merle Travis	*Beginning Fingerstyle Guitar*, Lou Manzi (Alfred/NGW#14099)	Acoustic steel-string Classical

Music is composed of three primary elements: harmony (the chord progression), melody (includes improvised solos) and rhythm (of the melody and the accompaniment—strumming and grooves). Learning about theory greatly demystifies music, enabling you to better comprehend its structure and how musical concepts intertwine. A great theory book written strictly for guitarists is *Theory for the Contemporary Guitarist*, by Guy Capuzzo (Alfred/NGW #16755).

CHORD KNOWLEDGE

The more chords you have at your disposal, the greater your ability to be resourceful and versatile. Many guitarists who have only been playing for a few years have concentrated solely on learning power chords (two-note chords with no 3rd) since they are used in so many contemporary songs. Although these chords are easy to learn and execute, they really are only the tip of the iceberg.

Chords fall under three categories:
1. **Power and Barre Chords.** Used extensively in rock (including alternative) and blues, these chords are transposable throughout the fretboard and the bass notes are emphasized.

2. **Open Chords.** Open chords are appropriately named since they usually have a few open strings in their construction and are mostly played in open position (the first four frets). They are played primarily in country, Latin, folk and rock ballads. Generally open chords are not transposable around the fretboard without a capo (unless transformed into barre chords).

3. **Extended Chords.** Of all the chords you will study, extended chords will require the most memory work. They are indispensable since they are needed for a wide range of styles. These chords are particularly important in jazz but are used sporadically in most other styles.

It is taken for granted that a session player has already mastered all the necessary chords. You will sometimes be called upon to play standard chords, and sometimes asked to be creative with different chord voicings (arrangements of notes in the chords). You can't afford to limit your chord knowledge. The guitar is an amazing instrument which allows you to construct every chord in many different ways—each time producing a small alteration in the sound. Explore all the possibilities at your disposal and be open to new and fresh ideas.

The following chart explores some of the basic chords you should learn. If you don't already know these, memorize them. Also train your ear to discern the differences in each of the chords. For example, learn to differentiate between the major, minor or dominant function of a chord. An ear training book, such as *Ear Training for the Contemporary Guitarist*, by Jody Fisher (Alfred/NGW #19370), will be helpful in this regard. In addition, look for ways to play each chord with a more interesting voicing (always in keeping with the context of the song). Don't just play chords in isolation. As soon as you learn a new chord, start playing it in a song. This way, you'll hear how it works with other chords.

Below are examples of chords you should know. This is a very limited sampling, so you should own some thorough chord resources, such as *The Ultimate Guitar Chord Bible* (NGW # 07-1083) and the *Guitar Chord Encyclopedia* (Alfred #4432).

OPEN CHORDS

Used extensively in folk and Latin music as well as rock ballads. There are many chords to learn but here are some common open major and minor chords. You should also learn dominant 7th and sus4 chords.

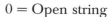

x = Mute this string.
0 = Open string

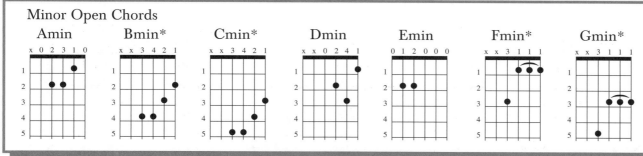

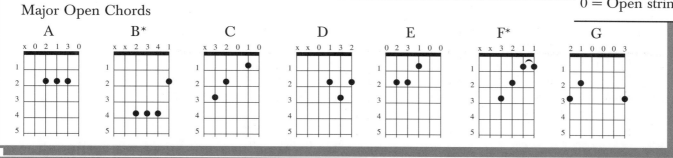

* Not technically open chords (they contain no open strings), these chord forms are, however, often used in conjunction with open chords, since they are found within the first five frets.

MOVABLE CHORDS—INCLUDING BARRE CHORDS, DOMINANT AND EXTENDED CHORDS

These are chords that can be used for all styles of music. Each one is fully transposable by simply moving the root to the desired note. As you will see, many chords without barres are still movable because they contain no open strings.

Chord Symbol Key

9	= Dominant 9	Maj9	= Major 9
11	= Dominant 11	min9	= Minor 9
13	= Dominant 13	Maj13	= Major 13
Maj7	= Major 7	min11	= Minor 11
min7	= Minor 7		

● = Root

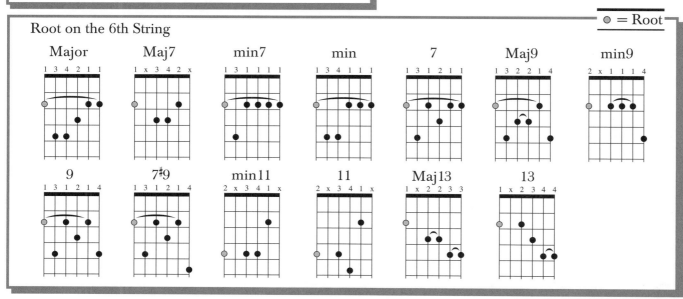

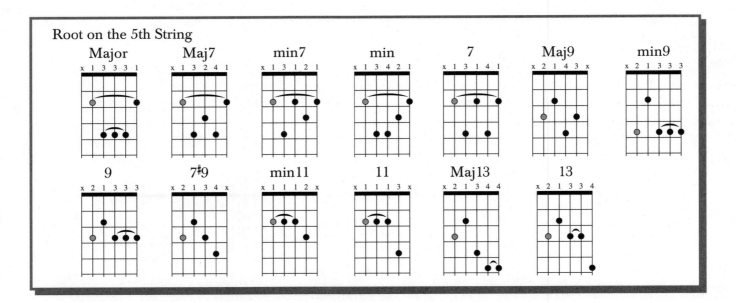

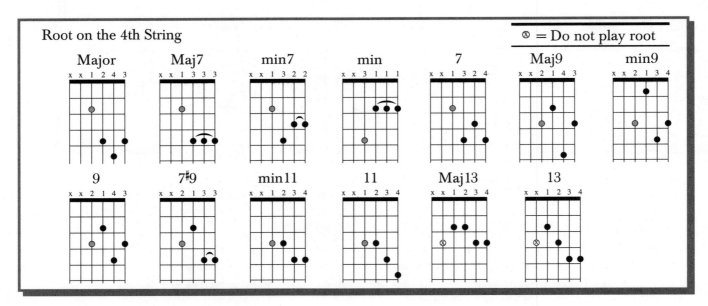

Be sure to make learning new chords a part of your regular practice routine, paying special attention to chords that seem specific to certain styles or artists. For example, Jimi Hendrix and Stevie Ray Vaughan frequently used the 7#9 chord in their songs.

CHORDS IN THE STUDIO

It is often possible to spice a tune up with chord enhancements. Every chord belongs to a certain family and, within these families, you can add various extensions and alterations on a chord with the same root as enhancements.

Here is a table of chords and possible enhancements.

CHORDS	ENHANCEMENTS
Major	Major Major 6 Major 6/9 Major 7 Major 9 Major 13 Major add 9
Minor	Minor Minor 6 Minor 7 Minor 7♭5 Minor 9 Minor 11 Minor 13
Dominant	7 9 11 13 Diminished Augmented
Altered	7♯5 7♭5 7♯9 7♭9
Suspended	Sus2 Sus4

In a studio situation, you need to get a feel for how much freedom you have to be creative before doing any fancy chord work. Many recording sessions may simply call for straight ahead chord progressions with no alterations, while others allow you to contribute your own ideas. Treat each situation individually. Some artists are better at songwriting than they are at making arrangements and may have a very basic approach to writing out their chords. If that is the case, you might be able to try some of your ideas. Sometimes just fiddling around with ideas as you're going over the chart may catch their ear. You'll also find that some artists know exactly what they want to hear and are pretty set on what they want you to record. Whatever you do, be sure to ask for permission before recording anything other than what is written in the chart.

Let's take a look at a basic chord progression you might run into.

Try enhancing the chords as follows.

CHAPTER 5
IMPROVISATION

There are several basic approaches to improvising (soloing). One is to memorize scales, riffs and arpeggios (broken chords) to use as source materials. This is often accompanied with copying ideas from other musicians and integrating what you learn into your own playing. Another approach is to improvise totally by ear and intuition. Most people oscillate between these approaches, playing some cool riffs and then using notes from a familiar scale (perhaps also borrowing some motives from the melody of the song) and mixing it into other ideas they hear in their head.

Learning to improvise well is a process that takes some time, practice and much patience. When first learning to improvise, it's a good idea to imitate a solo from one of your favorite guitarists. Try learning it by ear rather than from a written transcription. This way you are training your ear to to find notes on the guitar. Once you've learned a solo, work on mastering it so that it sounds technically polished. Play what you learn very slowly and accurately, so that you don't ingrain sloppy technique into your playing by attempting to play too fast before you're ready. Once you can play it slowly and accurately, work with a metronome to increase your speed incrementally.

Skilled improvisers take into account the context of the music over which they are soloing. When it comes to your own practicing or performances, you can experiment and try to push the envelope with new concepts and ideas. In a studio session, it's a little bit different. The studio is not be the ideal place to show off your lightning fast technique (unless of course that is what is requested). At all times, keep serving the song in the forefront. For example, if you are soloing over the changes of a country ballad, it is more appropriate to play melodically and with lots of emotion. On the other hand, if the tune you are recording is a fast blues, play more riffs with lots of bends, vibrato, hammer-ons and pull- offs. Sometimes underplaying is more effective than playing every single lick you know. The key is to choose tasteful ideas within the boundaries of the style in which you are soloing.

Technical Tip No. 21—Mastering Riffs

One of the best ways to perfect a riff or ideas you have learned is to set your metronome for half the tempo of the song. For example, if the tune is at 120 beats per minute, set the metronome to 60. Practice the solo at this speed until you perfect it, then raise the metronome to 62, then 64 and so on. Keep repeating this process until you reach the given tempo or even 10 to 20 beats per minute faster.

The biggest mistake novices make is to try and play at speeds that they are not yet comfortable with. If the notes aren't coming out smoothly and you are stumbling over them, it's a dead give-away that you are playing too fast. You are much better off learning something less complicated and making it sound polished than playing an amazing riff that sounds awkward.

CONCEPTS OF IMPROVISATION

PHRASING

Phrasing relates to the way we approach our soloing. It can be compared to speaking. You get an idea and you speak it, sometimes quickly, or slowly, at times pausing or even repeating ideas to get a point across. When you solo you are relating to the listener in the same manner. You are delivering musical concepts.

Each style of music demands a different approach to phrasing. A good way to understand this is to think about vocalists and how they sing their lyrics. Some vocalists are very smooth and elegant while others are more choppy and rough. It's mostly a personal thing, which evolves over time through experience and practice.

It is a good idea to spend some time singing along with what you play as you improvise. This will help you get more in touch with your playing and your solos will become more melodic.

BUILDING AN INTERESTING SOLO

As you play a solo, it's good not to give away everything all at once. Treat soloing like you are telling a story. Start with a little introduction, some easy riffs and then build up in the middle until you reach a climax right before the end. You may also want to add dynamics (variations in volume) and contrast using some lower notes than gliding up the higher register. Of course these are only suggestions and you'll need to try out different ideas to see what works best for you.

Listen to other players and try and analyze how they build their solos. Many great guitarists have their own signature soloing style and, once you've heard them a few times, you learn to recognize their "voice."

Even though we all learn from other guitarists, we naturally begin to develop our own style of improvising as we mature. Some studio guitarists come to a point where they are hired solely because people like the way they solo over a certain style of music. When you hear B.B. King, you learn to appreciate his simple but melodic style of blues improvising. Stevie Ray Vaughan, who also played the blues, was definitely more aggressive and riff oriented. They are both recognized for their own styles.

SCALES

Let's look at some of the popular scales listed in the chart on page 42.

THE MINOR PENTATONIC SCALE—FIVE PATTERNS

These scale patterns are all fully movable to any key by simply beginning on the tonic (shown with white circles) of the key you want. For example, to play pattern No. 1 in the key of A, start on the 5th fret, which will put the 6th string tonic on the note A. To play the same pattern in the key of B, start on the 7th fret, and so on.

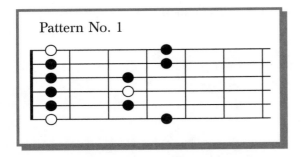

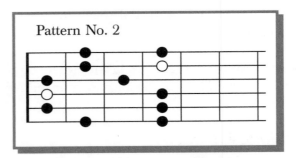

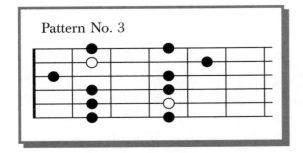

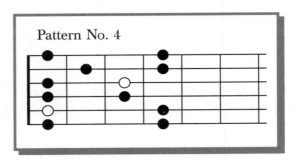

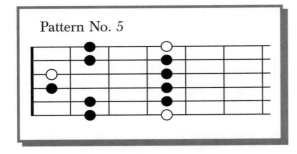

○ = Tonic

The major pentatonic scale patterns can be found by simply moving the minor pentatonic scale patterns down three frets. For example, if you are playing E Minor Pentatonic Scale Pattern No. 1 on the 12th fret, just move it down to the 9th fret to create an E Major Pentatonic Scale pattern. Remember, however, that an E tonic is still needed, so you will need to emphasize different fingers within the pattern to make it sound correct. This will be true with any minor pentatonic pattern that you change into major pentatonic with this method. **It is important that you know the names of the notes on the fretboard and are always aware of the locations of the tonic within any scale pattern.**

MODES OF THE MAJOR SCALE

A mode is a specific order of the notes in a scale. For example, a major scale played beginning and ending on the 2nd degree is the Dorian mode. Each mode has a specific character and works best over specific chords. For a complete study of modes, including those of the melodic minor and harmonic minor scales, check out *The Guitar Mode Encyclopedia*, by Jody Fisher (Alfred/NGW#4445) or *The Ultimate Guitar Scale Bible*, by Mark Dziuba (NGW#07-1009).

The modes of the major scale are by far the most commonly-used modes for improvisation. The chart below shows one useful pattern for each. Be sure to memorize them.

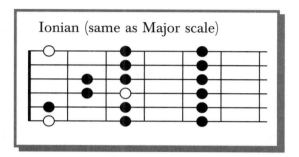

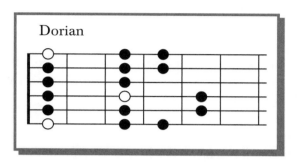

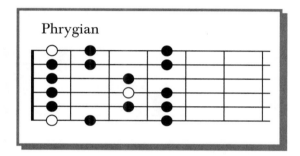

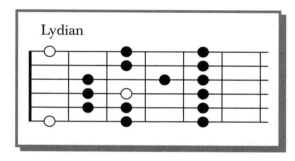

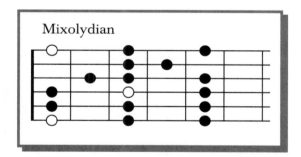

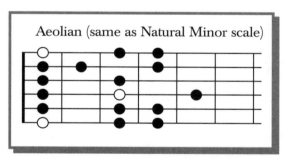

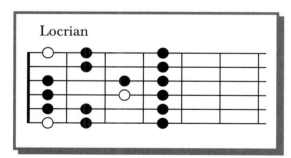

Scales are great guides for finding the notes which will work over a given progression. In most cases, the tonic of the scale should be the same as the key in which you are playing. As you become more advanced and are soloing over jazz progressions, you will start to pick scales that work with just a few chords, or even just one chord. This is called "making the changes." Resources such as *The Guitar Chord and Scale Finder*, by Jody Fisher (Alfred/NGW#14148) and *The Ultimate Guitar Scale Bible*, by Mark Dziuba (NGW# 07-1009), can help you learn which scales go with which chords.

Once you've memorized a scale pattern, immediately begin to solo with it, finding notes that seem to fit the progression over which you are playing. Make some backing tracks for yourself to practice playing over, or pick up some of the many play-along CDs available on the market, such as those in the Alfred/NGW *Stand Alone* series, which come in many styles. And don't forget to practice with your guitar plugged into your effects and your amp.

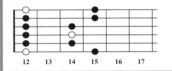

E Minor Pentatonic Scale: 12th Fret

It's helpful to build a vocabulary of licks for each style. These are short ideas that are usable in many different contexts. Let's start with a blues progression in E and a lick derived from an E Minor Pentatonic scale in Pattern No. 1 at the 12th fret. Blues players tend to use a lot of finger vibrato as well as bends throughout their solos. Each of the following progressions will be played twice; one with licks derived from the scale and the other so you can practice over it yourself. Be sure to also practice the chord progressions.

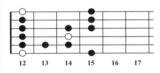

E Blues Scale

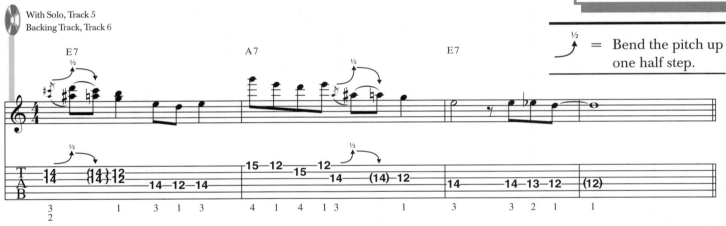

With Solo, Track 5
Backing Track, Track 6

½ = Bend the pitch up one half step.

Let's use the major pentatonic scale over the same progression by lowering the same scale pattern three frets (to the 9th fret). Even though this scale pattern looks exactly the same, it will sound quite different from how it did at the 12th fret. At the 12th fret in the key of E, it has a very bluesy sound. Playing it at the 9th fret gives it a major, brighter sound. Remember, you still need to emphasize the E tonic, which will fall under different fingers when the pattern is moved down in this manner. Notice that this lick uses slides (S), which are done by gliding a finger along the string to create a gliding sound between the notes.

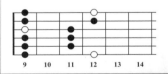

E Major Pentatonic Scale: 9th Fret

S/ = Slide
H = Hammer-on
P = Pull-off

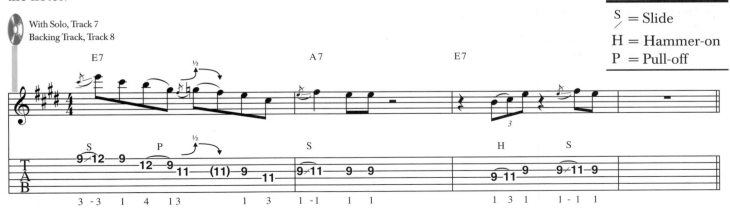

With Solo, Track 7
Backing Track, Track 8

The following Motown-style tune starts with the D Major Pentatonic scale and then moves into the G Dorian mode (over the G Minor chords). Your ear will always dictate when you need to move into a different scale. Also use your ear to determine which notes to emphasize and which ones to omit. Once you've learned a lot of scales, you will begin to sort out which are most appropriate for improvising over any given tune.

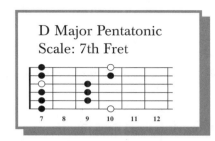

D Major Pentatonic
Scale: 7th Fret

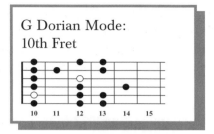

G Dorian Mode:
10th Fret

With Solo, Track 9
Backing Track, Track 10

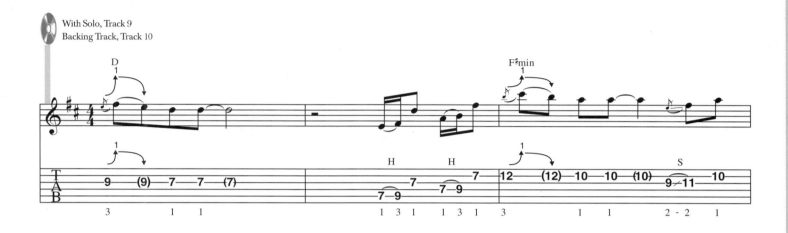

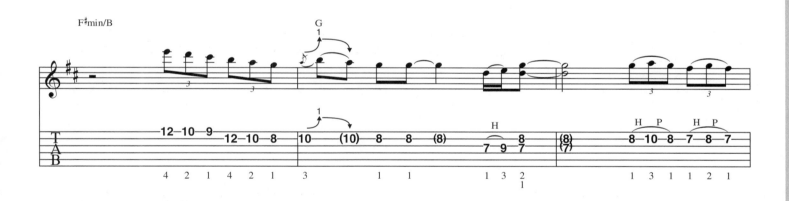

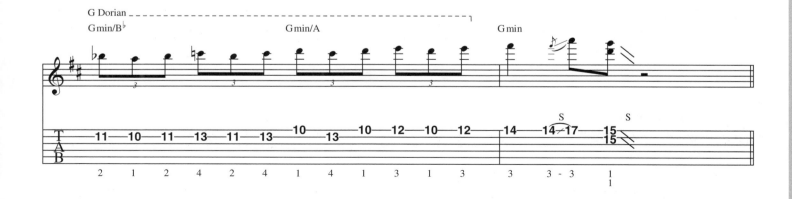

The next progression is a 12-bar blues in the style of B.B. King's "The Thrill is Gone," which is in the key of A Minor. The 12-bar blues is the most common progression used to play the blues, and is used for lots of rock music, too. To learn more about it, check out *Beginning Blues Guitar*, by David Hamburger (Alfred/NGW #20419).

It's a good idea to be able to differentiate between songs that are in major keys and songs that are in minor keys, because they each require a different approach while soloing. Major keys are generally brighter and happier sounding, while minor keys are darker and more melancholy. Getting to know some theory and doing some ear training will help you here.

You can use the A Aeolian mode to come up with some interesting licks in the key of A Minor. The A Minor Pentatonic scale is also a great scale to use over this progression. Try incorporating slides, pull-offs and hammer-ons, as well as bends and vibrato. This rock progression uses all of these techniques.

Notice how the solo is slow and melodic at first, building to a climax at the end.

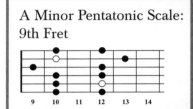

A Aeolian Mode:
5th Fret

A Minor Pentatonic Scale:
9th Fret

〰〰 = Vibrato

This eight-bar solo using the B♭ Major Pentatonic scale is very "up sounding" against this reggae-style progression. In typical reggae style, this solo is more percussive sounding and melodic than the previous solos. Also notice how the double stops (two notes played together by one player) in 6ths and 3rds add a harmonious twist to the solo.

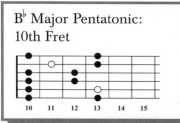

B♭ Major Pentatonic:
10th Fret

With Solo, Track 13
Backing Track, Track 14

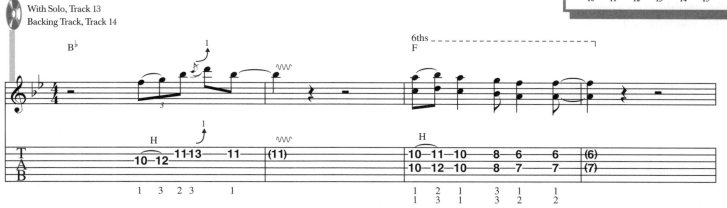

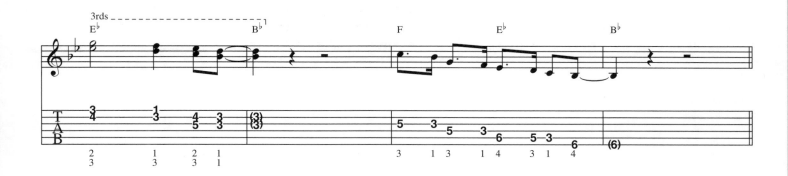

This example is in a country style using the C Major Pentatonic scale. For country music, you generally want to make your solo sound pretty melodic, perhaps even taking some of the vocal melody lines and weaving them into your solo. Bends are very appropriate for this style.

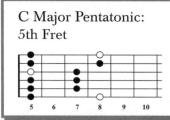

C Major Pentatonic:
5th Fret

With Solo, Track 15
Backing Track, Track 16

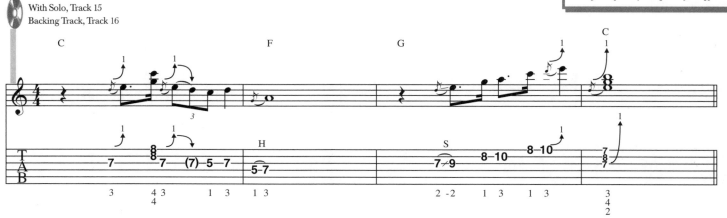

Unless you are known as a jazz guitarist you probably won't get called in to do a jazz session, but a producer may request for you to play your solo a little "jazzier." The following progression, in the style of the song "Black Orpheus," by Luiz Bonfá, uses the harmonic minor scale. Be sure to look up this scale in a theory or scale book and learn more about it.

To get a jazz feel you will need to swing the eighth notes; play them unevenly, giving more time to the first eighth note in each pair. Swing eighths sound like an eighth-note triplet with the first two eighth notes tied.

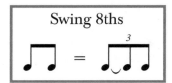

Note the use of octaves (measures 1, 3 and 5) and arpeggios (broken chords, measures 4 and 6) which are used extensively by jazz guitarists. Jazz players also sometimes use chords in their solos (as in measure 8). You will notice there are no bent strings or vibrato, which are more common to blues and rock. To get a rich, mellow jazz tone, try using a heavier gauge set of strings as well as a thicker, smaller pick which will make your attack quicker and fuller sounding. Most jazz guitarists use a guitar with double-coil pickups and decrease the treble on their amp and/or guitar for a smooth, mellow tone.

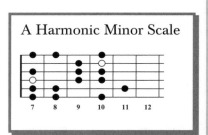

A Harmonic Minor Scale

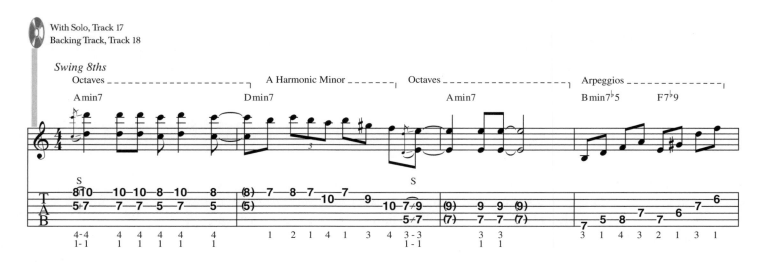

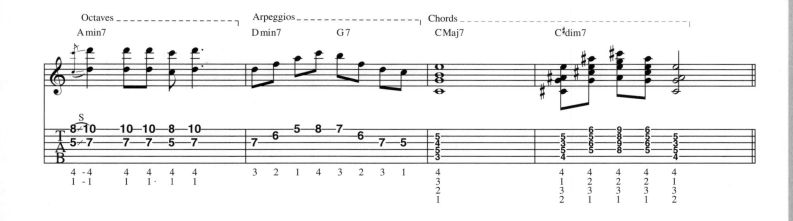

Here is an example of a funk-jazz progression. To play in any funk-based style, you need to keep the feel of the rhythm strongly in mind. The soloing here is a little more percussive. This example uses the F Mixolydian mode.

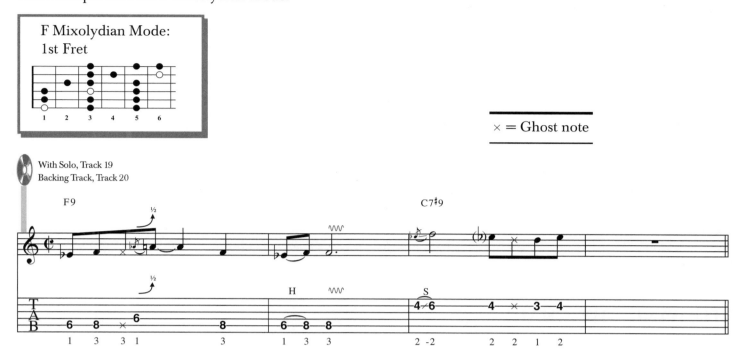

Let's take a look at a lick one might play on an acoustic guitar. The D Aeolian mode sounds great over this progression. This lick is in the 12th position, so it would work best on a guitar with a cutaway.

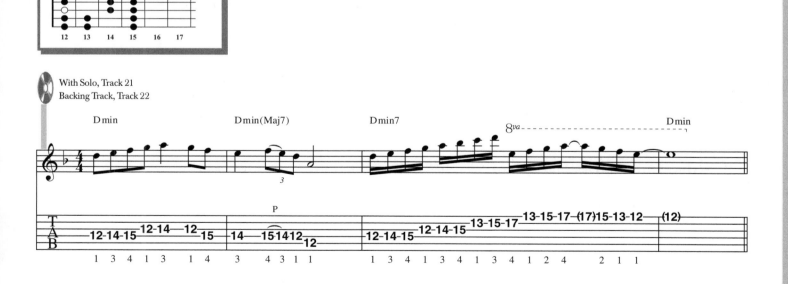

CHAPTER 6
READING CHARTS

More often than not, when you go into a recording session, you will be handed a music chart (also called a lead sheet) of some sort, either printed or handwritten, for the song you will be recording. The first thing you need to do is familiarize yourself with it and identify any trouble spots or areas that seem unclear. Play through the chart to get the general idea of how it is constructed. If you are unsure of something, or something seems odd, inquire about it before recording begins.

If you plan on making a career as a studio musician, good reading skills are required. You should practice your reading chops as a part of your regular practicing routine. Try reading something every day and always attempt to sight-read (reading once through only). You don't necessarily have to be a phenomenal reader to start taking gigs, but you will need to work on this area so you can handle any chart put in front of you. Check out some of the guitar sight-reading books that are available, such as *Sight-Reading for the Contemporary Guitarist,* by Tom Dempsey (Alfred/NGW #21954).

STUDYING THE CHART

These are things you should look for in a chart:

1. **Tempo**—This is the speed at which the song is to be played. You may see a marking like this:

   $\quad \quad \downarrow = 105$

   This indicates a speed of 105 beats per minute. You can check this with a metronome. Sometimes there is no tempo but you will see a tempo instruction, such as "Slow and Rhythmic," or "Medium with a Lift." If it's not clear, don't be afraid to ask.

2. **Time Signature**—Be sure to take note of this sign, such as $\frac{4}{4}$, which appears at the beginning of every chart. While most music you play will be in $\frac{4}{4}$, others will come up now and then. Make sure you are well-versed on this topic, as each time signature has its own specific feel. Any good method book will be helpful in this area.

3. **Key Signature**—The key signature appears after the treble clef ? to let you know the key in which you will be playing. This is an important element since it determines which notes are sharp or flat in the song as well as in which key to play your scales.

4. **Style**—On the top left-hand side of most charts, you will find an indication of the style of the song. For example, it may say "Country Ballad" or "Blues Shuffle," etc.

5. **Dynamics**—Look out for markings that indicate changes in the volume of the song. Some of the most important dynamic indications are:

p	*Piano*	Soft
mf	*Mezzo forte*	Medium
f	*Forte*	Loud
(crescendo hairpin)	*Crescendo*	Getting gradually louder
(decrescendo hairpin)	*Decrescendo*	Getting gradually softer

6. **Form**—Every song has a structure which you will need to know. Most popular songs have these parts:

   a. **Intro**: This is the introduction to the song. Usually anywhere from four to eight bars of instrumental material.

   b. **Verse**: There are often several verses. This is the part of the song that tells the story. The melody is the same each time, but the lyrics change.

   c. **Chorus**: The chorus is usually the hook or catchy part of the tune, and imparts the main idea. It is usually the same each time.

   d. **Prechorus**: This section is before the chorus and normally of short duration.

   e. **Bridge**: A contrasting, transitional section. Sometimes used to add variety, lengthen a song or solo over.

7. **Repeat signs**—Watch out for sections of a song that need to be repeated, which will be marked with these signs

:‖ Left-facing repeat. Go back to the beginning or the last right-facing repeat and play again.

‖: Right-facing repeat. When you get to a left-facing repeat, come back here and play the section between the repeats again.

8. **Difficult sections**—Make sure you examine the chart for any unfamiliar chords or notation that seems challenging to play. Run through that area a few times so you get it down pat before recording.

9. **Rests**—Don't forget to factor in any rests. These are areas where you are not playing. Could be a few bars or a whole section.

10. **Special Instructions**—Be aware of roadmap-type instructions, even where you are soloing. These may include indications such as *D.C. al Coda*. (*Da Capo al Coda* means play from the beginning up to the coda sign Ꝋ, then skip to the coda. A coda is an ending section.)

CHORD SYMBOLS

Following are a few of the chord name abbreviations you may see. This chart uses an F root for each chord.

Major .... F	Minor 7 .... Fmin7, Fm7, or F-7
Minor .... Fmin, F-, Fm	Dominant 7: F7
Diminished .... Fdim, F°	Diminished 7: .... Fdim7, F°7
Augmented .... Faug, F+	Suspended 4th: .... F7sus4, Fsus
Major 7 .... FMaj7, Fmaj7, FM7, Fma7	Altered Chords: ...... F7♯5, F7♭5, F7♯9

Symbols for altered chords always show the extensions (notes above the 7th) you will actually be using. Sometimes they will be surrounded by parentheses, for example: F7(♯9).

There are many other symbols you may run into but these are the most common ones.

FOLLOWING THE CHART

Being able to follow a chart, even while you aren't playing, is a vital aspect of reading. Let's say your job is to play only a few lines between bars 17 and 24. You will need to be able to follow the chart as the song is going along and know exactly when bar 17 arrives and then keep track of things, so that you stop at bar 24. The best way to accomplish this is to count the beats and bars, like this: 1–2–3–4, 2–2–3–4, 3–2–3–4, and so on. It is also helpful to look ahead periodically, staying aware of what's coming while still being conscious of your present position. This takes a little bit of practice.

After a while you will be able to quickly scan through a chart and zero in on any potential challenges. To practice reading, try and obtain as many different charts as possible. You may get into a situation where a tune is poorly charted or illegible. Be sure to remain professional and work out any bugs with the producer.

READING CHARTS: EXAMPLE NO. 1

The first tune we will be looking at is a 12-bar blues in the style of Eric Clapton's "Before You Accuse Me." You have been called into the studio to record the guitar parts and play a solo. Let's take a look at some of the things you will want to be aware of in this chart.

1. The first thing you should look at is the style of the tune. In this case the indication at the top left is "Fast Rock Blues."

2. The tempo, ♩ = 140, is indicated right under the style and the time signature, which is $\frac{4}{4}$.

3. The key signature is E Major, which is indicated with the four sharps (F♯, C♯, G♯ and D♯). If you look through the chart, you will notice that it modulates (changes keys) twice. The first modulation is at bar 13, to the key of F Major, and the second is at bar 25, to the key of G. You can use the minor pentatonic scale to solo in each of these keys; in the key of E Major, use the E Minor Pentatonic scale; in the key of F Major, use the F Minor Pentatonic scale.

> **Technical Tip No. 22—Working with a Metronome**
>
> *It's very valuable to invest some time in working with a metronome. Not only will it help you understand tempo, but it will also help you play in time when practicing. Some guitarists don't do this and it's evident in their rhythm playing, as well as their improvising.*

4. You will see repeat signs throughout this chart.
   • The first left-facing repeat sign appears at bar 14, indicating that you should return to the right-facing repeat sign at bar 3 and play to bar 14 again.
   • The next left-facing repeat sign is at bar 26, indicating that you should return to the right-facing repeat at bar 15 and play to 26 again.

5. The special instructions that pertain to you are found at the intro, bar 3, 15 and 37. These give you specific instructions about what to play. At the intro it says to play a guitar fill. This means to play a lick of some kind. Most blues players have a few memorized intro licks that they can pull out of the hat as needed. See *Mastering Blues Guitar* by Wayne Riker (Alfred/NGW #8234) for ideas for intro and ending fills. Bar 15 lets you know that you will be soloing over this section the second time. At bar 37 (the second time around) your instructions are to play an outro (ending) fill to the end.

DON'T EXCUSE ME

READING CHARTS: EXAMPLE NO. 2

The following chart is a little trickier to read. It's in the style of Jose Feliciano's "Affirmation." You have been called in to lay down the rhythm guitar tracks and take a solo on the second head. A saxophone player will play the melody.

Let's dissect this chart:

1. The style is Medium Funk-Rock. Use single-coil pickups and play a funky rhythm.

2. The Tempo is ♩ = 108 and the time signature is represented by this symbol c. This means common time, which is another name for $\frac{4}{4}$.

3. The key signature has two sharps (F♯ and C♯) so you are in the key of D Major. Most of the chords in this song are taken from this key. For soloing, you can use the D Major scale (or the E Dorian mode over the E Minor chords).

4. First, the group plays the head. The head is the melody of the song. This song is in an AAB form, which means the A section (the first section, notice the section markings at bars 1 and 23), is repeated twice. The bracket marked with a "1" at bar 11 is called a first ending.

The second A section starts again at bar 1, but this time you play up to the end of bar 10 and then skip to bar 17 (this is the second ending marked with a "2").

At bar 23 there is a "B" symbol indicating you are in the B section of the song, which continues until bar 30.

5. The special instruction at bar 30, *D.C. al Coda*, tells you that once you have played the head through a few times (ask the producer how many times), you will go back to the top and play to the coda sign at bar 9. Instead of playing bar 9, jump to bar 31 (at bottom of the page where there is another coda sign) and play this section. Notice the instruction at the end, telling you to keep repeating until the music fades (there are repeat signs at bars 31 and bar 34).

6. Since you have been hired as the rhythm guitarist for this song, you will record your guitar playing a few times through the head). Chances are bass and drum tracks were put down before you arrived and you will play your rhythm part on top of those pre-recorded tracks.

7. Once your rhythm part has been recorded, you are asked to solo over the second time through the head. You will need to follow the chart closely as you solo and be sure not to lose your place. By the time you have to record your solo, you'll probably have a good feel for the form of the song.

APPLICATION

NASHVILLE NUMBERING SYSTEM

The Nashville Numbering System was created in 1955 by Neal Matthews of the Jordanaires (a famous quartet of singers who backed up Elvis Presley) as a means of saving time and costs in the studio. Its popularity has spread worldwide and is practiced by amateurs and professional studio musicians alike. The concept is quite simple: a number is assigned to each chord in a key, and the numbers are used instead of chord names or symbols.

For example, the chords belonging to the key of C Major have a corresponding number above them:

1	2	3	4	5	6	7
C	Dmin	Emin	F	G7	Amin	B°

Using this system, a song in C Major with the chords C, Emin, G7 would be written in a chart like this: 1, 3-, 5.

Let's take a look at how a Nashville Numbering chart would be written.

3- = 3 is a minor chord

DIANNE'S DREAM

$\frac{4}{4}$ Ballad	Key of E
I	1 45 5 5
V	2- 1 1 1
CH	1 5 1 1
	1 5 1 1
V	2- 1 1 1
Solo	1 45 5 5
CH	1 5 1 1
	1 5 1 1
CH	1 5 1 1
	1 5 1 1
Outro	1 45 5 5

CHART ANALYSIS

1. The first thing we see from this chart is that it is in standard $\frac{4}{4}$ time and that it is a *ballad* (slow song).

2. After the title, we see that the key is in E (E Major).

3. Before the first set of numbers we see an "I" which is short for "Introduction." Each number is separated by a space which indicates one bar of music. Therefore the intro has 4 bars of music. When there are two chords in a bar, the two numbers appear next to each other as in the "45" in the Intro, Solo and Outro sections. It is usually safe to assume that the chord change occurs on beat 3 of the bar. Since this is in the key of E Major, the numbers 1, 45, 5, 5 represent E, A, B, B, B (see the chart on page 65).

4. The next section is the Verse (V), which also has four bars. The "2" has a "-" slash symbol beside it indicating it is a minor chord. This can sometimes appear "2m."

5. After the Verse is the Chorus (CH), which has eight bars.

6. This is followed by a four-bar solo.

7. The next two sections are repeats of the Chorus.

8. Finally, we have the Outro indicating the end of the tune.

This system makes it easier to transpose (change the key of) any song. For example, if you are in a studio situation and the vocalist is having a problem singing in the original key of a song—maybe it's too high, for example—you might be asked to lower the key. Sometimes just dropping the key by one tone allows the vocalist to sing with more ease. If you have already memorized the chords of the 12 major keys (the chart below), you will automatically know which chords to be play and won't have to go through the whole process of figuring out each one individually.

The advantage to this system is its simplicity. The disadvantage is that you cannot write individual notes for specific passages of music. This works best in a situation where the musicians are used to playing these kind of charts, and have memorized the 12 major keys so they can recall them instantly.

Below are the chords of the 12 major keys related to the Nashville Numbering system.

KEY	1	2-	3-	4	5	6-	7
C	C	Dmin	Emin	F	G	Amin	Bdim
D♭	D♭	E♭min	Fmin	G♭	A♭	B♭min	Cdim
D	D	Emin	F#min	G	A	Bmin	C#dim
E♭	E♭	Fmin	Gmin	A♭	B♭	Cmin	Ddim
E	E	F#min	G#min	A	B	C#min	D#dim
F	F	Gmin	Amin	B♭	C	Dmin	Edim
G♭	G♭	A♭min	B♭min	C♭	D♭	E♭min	Fdim
G	G	Amin	Bmin	C	D	Emin	F#dim
A♭	A♭	B♭min	Cmin	D♭	E♭	Fmin	Gdim
A	A	Bmin	C#min	D	E	F#min	G#dim
B♭	B♭	Cmin	Dmin	E♭	F	Gmin	Adim
B	B	C#min	D#min	E	F#	G#min	A#dim

CHAPTER 7
SLIDE GUITAR AND ALTERNATE TUNING

A lot of guitarists enjoy playing slide because of its ability to imitate the human voice. Although playing slide is not necessarily mainstream, it is still held in high regard in many circles.

At one point or another in your career you will be asked to play slide guitar in a recording session. Work on acquiring at least an elementary slide technique. Take some time to develop a smooth flow with your slide-hand, practicing good intonation. Unlike the guitar where the pitch is pre-determined by frets, you will need to use your ear (and eyes) to find the right pitch. You should also accumulate a few licks, tricks of the trade and get a few different styles under your belt.

Some great slide guitarists to investigate are Ry Cooder, Bonnie Raitt, Duane Allman and even Eric Clapton.

EQUIPMENT YOU WILL NEED
GUITAR

When it comes to guitars used for side, you definitely don't need to spend a lot of money. Actually, a trashy old guitar that doesn't get much use would be a good candidate. This is one area in which having a high action is actually recommended, since it allows for a smooth gliding along the string without fret interference. In any case, it is best to have a guitar set up specifically for slide, since the lower action most players usually prefer for normal playing will not be good for slide.

Slide is also referred to as "bottleneck" because many early slides were homemade from the broken necks of beer bottles.

You can play slide guitar using regular tuning, which can be a little tricky or by using an alternate (or open) tuning (see page 68).

Metal slides for playing lap or pedal steel can also be used if your guitar is resting flat on your lap, but most slide players play with their guitars in the normal position.

SLIDES

There are several types of slides available. They are steel, glass, or ceramic and come in either full or half-length. Each type produces a different tone so you will have to experiment to see which one suits you best. They also come in different sizes, so try it on before buying one.

TIPS ON USING A SLIDE

1. When playing slide, make sure your slide hand is not slanted or you will have intonation problems. The hand should be at a right angle to the neck, so that the slide is exactly parallel to the frets.

2. Unlike playing regular guitar, the slide rests on the strings directly on top of the fret rather than behind it.

3. Don't press too hard or you will rub against the frets and create buzzes.

4. Aim for smooth, clean transitions as you move up and down the strings. Unlike playing regular guitar, where the frets determine your pitch, using your ear is essential for playing in tune.

5. Slide vibrato is an important, commonly used technique. You can get a more pronounced and quicker vibrato with a slide than in normal playing.

6. You can experiment with flat-wound or half-wound strings if you are getting too many rattles and other noises.

Technical Tip No. 23—Muting

In order to play single notes with the slide, you will need to master muting with your right hand. Use your index finger to play the desired string and rest the other fingers as well as the thumb on the other strings to keep them from ringing. Practicing this technique until you get a clean sound is the key to playing the slide successfully.

OPEN AND ALTERNATE TUNINGS

Standard guitar tuning (E, A, D, G, B, E) has been around for centuries but is by no means the only way to tune a guitar. Any other tuning falls into the general category of alternate tunings. These tunings emerged from the slide guitar playing of early Delta blues masters, and continue to be used in various styles.

Many folk artists work solely with alternate tunings since they lend themselves well to fingerstyle guitar playing. Check out artists such as Ani DiFranco, Adrian Legg or Michael Hedges to hear great playing in innovative of alternate tunings. For a more in-depth study of this subject, see *Introducing Alternate Tunings*, by Mark Dziuba (Alfred/NGW #14197).

Alternate tunings normally fall into one of two categories.

1. Open Tunings. The strings comprise the notes of a chord when either strummed open or barred.

2. Variation Tunings. Some of the strings are in standard tuning and others are changed. The most commonly used tunings in this category include:

   1. Drop D Tunings

   2. Modal Tunings

   3. Minor (or Crossnote) Tunings

> ### Technical Tip No. 24—Alternate Tuning
>
> *You may want to make it a habit to choose the tunings that are tuned down from standard pitch rather than the other way around. This way you lessen the chances of breaking strings from too much string tension.*

There are other assorted, more unusual tunings. For slide guitar, you will mostly use the open tunings D, E, G and A. For examples of Open D tuning listen to Ry Cooder. Bonnie Raitt uses the Open A tuning in most of her tunes.

Open G tuning is probably the most popular slide tuning. (The notes in parentheses can be used to tune the next higher string.)

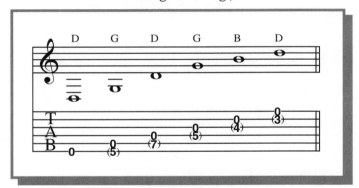

Assuming you may want to go back and forth between slide and regular playing when in this tuning, you will need to rework your chord shapes. For example, here are three common major chord shapes in Open G.

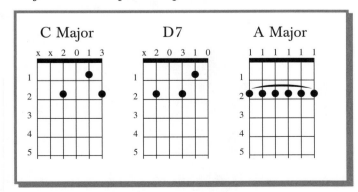

ALTERNATE TUNING CHART

Note: Arrows point in the direction that strings need to be returned, up or down.

↓ = Tune down
↑ = Tune up

STRINGS	6 E	5 A	4 D	3 G	2 B	1 E
Open	Open tuning refers to tuning the guitar to a chord.					
G (Spanish)	D↓	G↓	D	G	B	D↓
C	C↓	G↓	C↓	G	C↑	E
E	E	B↑	E↑	G#↑	B	E
D	D↓	A	D	F#↓	A↓	D↓
A	E	A	E↑	A↑	C#↑	E
Drop D	Drop D tunings are very popular and easy to apply. Very little retuning is necessary.					
D1	D↓	A	D	G	B	E
D2	D↓	A	D	G	A↓	E
D3	D↓	A	D	F#↓	B	D↓
D4	D↓	A	D	E↓	A↓	E
D5	D↓	A	D	G	B	D↓
Modal	These are similar to open tunings and have an ambiguous, suspended quality. They work best for fingerstyle guitar playing.					
D	D↓	A	D	G	A↓	D↓
G Sawmill	D↓	G↓	D	G	C↑	D↓
Minor	Also called crossnote tunings, these tunings have a minor, melancholy sound.					
D	D↓	A	D	F↓	A↓	D↓
E	E	B↑	E↑	G	B	E

PART 3—THE HOME STUDIO
CHAPTER 8
CREATING YOUR OWN STUDIO

We are living in an incredible time, with new technology opening up phenomenal opportunities which were previously non-existent. With the low cost of technology, there is no reason why any serious musician (or hobbyist for that matter) can't build their own home-based studio. You may not aspire to being a producer or engineer but simply want to record your own material. There is no better time than the present.

SETTING UP YOUR STUDIO

First of all, you need a room or a section of a room where you will be able to put your equipment. Make sure you are set up close enough to an output so you can have easy access and not trip over the wires. The basic requirements for your setup are:

1. A flat table or desk

2. Electrical outputs

3. Telephone or cable hookup (if you will be using a computer and downloading from the Internet)

4. Good light source (lamps, etc.)

5. Guitars, stands, music stands and a mic stand with microphone (if recording voice or acoustic guitars)

6. Equipment of choice (computer, digital studio or portastudio)

Chances are you already own a lot of this equipment. The main thing you need to concern yourself with is the recording gear.

DIRECT RECORDING

There are two approaches you can take for recording your guitar in your own studio. You can either go direct (via digital or analog) or use microphones (vocals, acoustic guitars, amps). Let's look into direct recording first (microphone recording is covered in Chapter 9, page 84). Direct recording is done by plugging your guitar into some type of preamp and then into the line-input of your computer soundcard (or mixer, if you are using one).

There are many advantages to going direct for recording your guitar. The most obvious advantage is sheer convenience. When going direct, you don't have to worry about using an amp or mic. Since you will probably be using headphones or small monitors to hear your sound, you will not have to worry about distracting others around you. One great benefit of direct recording is the absence of noise or hiss from amplifiers or other sources; it is basically a noise-free signal, which makes your recording a lot cleaner.

In digital recording, there is the added advantage of storing and recalling previously saved settings. For example, if you added a reverb with some compression from the onboard software in your computer, you can keep the exact levels (presets) for the next time you record. This is difficult when working with amps and mics, which seem to be affected by the simplest alteration.

Also, with today's advancing technology, not only has recording gear become very affordable, but also much smaller, allowing you to carry equipment away from your main studio. And because of the no-noise element, you can record almost anywhere you go without concern of people complaining about the volume.

The disadvantage of direct recording is the same as mentioned earlier with regard to digital modeling amps (page 30). You just can't reproduce with exact authenticity what comes from the straight-ahead setup of guitar, effects and amp. However, many guitarists continue to buy digital equipment in record numbers. If you have a limited budget and simply want to have your own studio for demos and preproduction, direct recording is an easy compromise. Some bands have gotten the attention of record companies with a well-produced demo made with a simple portastudio.

Technical Tip No. 25—Room Reverb

Most studios have little natural reverb or echo in the room. Too much reverb will color the sound of your recordings. It's best to have a "dry" room response and add reverb digitally (or from your amp). To check the level of reverb in your room, simply clap your hands a few times. If there is not much echo, it is a better environment than if it sounds like a large hall or a washroom. Adding carpeting or thick curtains will help deaden the sound. Some rooms actually have just the right amount of natural reverb without requiring adjustments, such as rooms with wooden floors.

FOUR-TRACK RECORDERS

Four-track recorders, also called portastudios, became popular in the early 1980s. They consist of a mixer into which you can record directly and then bounce your tracks (bouncing refers to combining two or more tracks together into a single track). Standard portastudios use a tape cassette as the recording media. The tape device has variable speeds which allows you to run it faster for better recording quality. Because this tape records quicker than regular tape players, you can't then just play the cassette on a regular cassette player. Once you get a good take, you must then mix down the tracks to a regular cassette recorder, DAT (digital audio tape), or two-track reel to reel.

Believe it or not, at the time of this writing, portastudios are still an excellent investment. They have been greatly improved since the 1980s and many reputable companies, such as Yamaha and Roland, still make them. You can even use virtual tracking to combine your four-track and midi signals. This is done by assigning one of the tracks to synch up with a sequencer using a time code (such as SMPTE*) which will then be used to control any MIDI instruments you may want to run through it. This will allow midi sounds to be played or recorded without occupying any of the tracks, since it's the timecode which controls the midi sequencer. MIDI instruments may be keyboards or synth sounds such as horns, drums, piano, organ, etc. You could also link up a drum machine or loops for your bed tracks (foundational tracks). The remaining tracks could be used for rhythm guitar and lead as well as a vocal track.

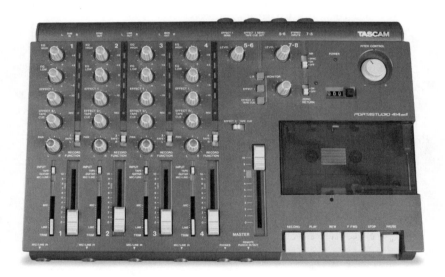

*Four-track recorders are versatile, inexpensive and can
yield fairly good results.*

The downside of these units is they still record on cassette tape, which means that every time you bounce a track onto another track, there will be a generational loss (a loss of quality from being an additional step away from the initial recording). Also, cassette tape, due to its small width, does not allow the greatest tonal quality.

* SMPTE is short for Society for Motion Picture and TV Engineers time code, an eight-digit code for numbering each frame on videotape, in the form HH:MM:SS:FF (hours, minutes, seconds, frames).

MINIDISC OR ZIP DISK

The upgrade for a portastudio is the minidisc recorder. Minidisc recorders look very similar to portastudios but are digital. Operating in the digital domain allows you to edit and undo takes with more ease than recording on cassette. You can also move pieces of your recorded takes around to different sections within the song. The main problem with minidiscs is their memory is stored on discs such as a Zip disk. These disks have storage limitations, therefore you will have to dump the material to another storage device in short intervals after only a few tunes.

Minidiscs are a step up from portastudios and allow you to record in a digital format.

EIGHT-TRACK RECORDERS

The two formats available for eight-tracks are reel-to-reel and MDM (modular digital multi-tracks).

REEL-TO-REEL

Reel-to-reels have been around the recording scene since the 1940s. There are two- and four-track formats but the professional ones start at eight and go as high as 24. Although somewhat obsolete since the introduction of hard disk recording, they are still being made by companies such as TEAC and TASCAM, to name just two. The attraction of tape has always been its analog warmth which was difficult, until fairly recently, to duplicate in the digital domain. With the advent of inexpensive tube pre-amps, either as hardware or software, warm tape-quality sound has become more accessible in the digital domain.

A reel-to-reel recorder uses a double-reel design where the tape (referred to as magnetic tape) goes from one reel through tape heads onto a second reel. The tape comes in quarter-, half-, 1- and 2-inch sizes. The wider the tape, the better the quality of the recording.

The disadvantages to using reel-to-reel recording machines are their bulk and problems maintaining the tape heads (wear-and-tear), tape damage and signal-to-noise ratio (the ratio of good sound to unwanted noise).

All in all, the digital format is making reel-to-reels an antiquated technology, but they can still be useful and are very cheap to buy second-hand.

Reel-to-reel recorders are still available today but have lost popularity since the advent of hard-disk recording.

MODULAR DIGITAL MULTI-TRACKS

MDMs (modular digital multi-tracks) have replaced the reel-to-reel in many studios. They still use tape as the media, which means they are linear machines—once you have recorded onto them you can't edit parts (cut and paste), unlike minidiscs. Because an MDM uses a tape running over a tape head, it will have the same drawbacks as the reel-to-reel (tape damage and wear-and-tear of the head). Because they are considered deck units, they don't have their own built-in mixers. Therefore you also need to have an external mixer.

One good feature of MDMs is they can be synced up with other MDMs to create more tracks. For instance, if you sync together three units you will have the equivalent of 24 tracks.

Modular Digital Multi-track units have all but replaced reel-to-reels.

STAND-ALONE HARD-DISK—MIXER OR NO MIXER

The next evolution in digital recorders is the stand-alone, also called workstation hard disk. These devices are similar to MDMs but use discs rather than tape as the media. Also, you still need to have a mixer since there isn't one built into this unit. Since it has a disc, you will run into the same problems as with minidisk units: storage limitations. One must frequently dump the recorded material onto another medium, such as Zip disks. Stand-alones are advantageous in that, unlike MDMs, you have editing capabilities and quicker access.

The hard-disk recorders look a lot like MDMs but store their memory to disk instead of tape.

DAWs (short for digital audio workstations) are also stand-alones but come with a built-in digital mixer. They have their own onboard effects, CD burners and other features. An example of a DAW is the Yamaha AW-16G 16-Track DAW, which has a built-in sampler and CD burner. Some models, such as TASCAM's US428 USB series use Cubasis VST audio recording and MIDI sequencing software. These units are very portable and work well in small environments.

Digital audio workstations are stand-alone units that include a built-in mixer.

MIXING

Once you have recorded all of your tracks, you will need to mix your material down to stereo before going to the next stage (mastering). Mixing is a skill that takes time to master. You can either mix yourself, or hire an expert to do it for you. Many musicians take their recorded tracks to a professional studio and get their mix done by an engineer. Depending on how many tunes you are recording, this can be costly.

This is a huge topic worthy of its own book, but following are some general points to guide you.

After having recorded all your music, you need to combine all of your tracks together to create the final mixdown. To give any song a polished sound, you must deal with:

1. **Panning**. Putting certain tracks to the left, center or right within the listening sphere.

2. **EQ**. Adjusting the treble, midrange and bass individually and globally for a balanced sound.

3. **Depth**. Adding reverb or echo to create the illusion of space.

4. **Compression**. Used to avoid extreme dynamic peaks.

5. **Effects**. Adding color to enhance the sound of the instruments.

When deciding which format to mix to, first decide:

1. **Will you be making a lot of copies (dubs)?** For many copies (over 25), mixing to DAT (digital audio tape recorder, a two-track recorder predominantly used for stereo mixdowns) is best.

2. **What kind of quality are you looking for?** If it's only for your own reference, try mixing down to cassette. If you are using a digital format and want to warm up your sound, you could first mix down to a two-track reel-to-reel and then to DAT.

Technical Tip No. 26—Mixing Monitors

If you do your own mixing, you should purchase near-field monitors, which are designed to produce a flat, non-colored reproduction of your recorded music. They provide a true representation of your mix, enabling you to tell if there is too much bass or treble. This way, when you listen to your music in another listening environment, the EQ will be more accurate. Once you've got your mix, try playing it in different places to see how it sounds. For example, try it in your car, or in your home stereo system. If you're not happy with the different results you will need to remix.

MASTERING

Mastering is another phase of the recording process that takes skill to undertake. Mastering prepares your recording to be duplicated.

There are many computer software packages that allow you to master your own mixes or you can hire a professional to do it for you. If you are using your recording for your own purposes only, or if you are just using it to get gigs around your area, you don't need to master. Mastering should be done when you want to present your music in the most professional manner possible, either to sell to the public or to send to a record company.

It is important to know exactly what mastering will do for you. Mastering:

1. **Evens out volume levels between songs**. This is also done for television programs so that when you are changing channels, one station is not louder or softer than the other. In the same way, you don't want a heavy tune to blast out of your speakers and then your ballads to be barely heard. The aim is to get each song to the same volume level.

2. **Zeros in on trouble spots and allows you to tweak them, but only to a certain degree**. Even though you use EQ on each individual track and on your mixdown, you may still want to do some EQing while mastering. At this stage, however, you can only do a global EQ, such as brightening or adding more bass to the whole mix.

3. **Allows you to do a certain amount of processing**. For example, you may have a vocal that seems to jump out of the mix at a certain frequency in a way you didn't notice during mixdown. By using compression, you can go in and bring down the range of dynamics in that frequency to create a more balanced sound.

4. **Adds a preset gap of two to four seconds between each tune**. This is an important aspect of mastering as well as a common practice.

5. **Gives your recording an overall polished sound and flow**. It allows everything to flow together without too many peaks or dives.

Technical Tip No. 27—Mastering

There's an expression in the recording industry that goes like this, "You can't polish a turd." Basically, it means that if your recorded tracks and mix are not of superior quality, you can't expect miracles at the mastering stage. Only so much improvement can be accomplished as your product is mastered. The general rule is one should expect about a 10% improvement for your product.

VIRTUAL STUDIOS

Virtual or computer-based studios are quickly becoming the norm. You can put together a virtual studio for half the cost of a traditional home studio. A few thousand dollars will get you a computer system with almost everything you need built in. If you are just beginning on your recording journey, you may want to start out with the basic recording gear as previously discussed and build up to a total virtual studio as your budget allows. Any skills you learn from using external gear such as minidiscs or computer-based hard-disk units will be transferable to a virtual set up. The only difference is that you are dealing with software that takes the place of the external equipment.

The real advantage to virtual studios is that they have software that will handle all your recording needs including effects, playback capabilities, MIDI, multi-tracks and automated mixers. There is very little you will need outside of your computer except for a few external devices. Once you have done all your recording, mixing and mastering internally, you can even duplicate your own CDs for distribution when needed.

If you have a band, you may want to put aside some cash for a powerful computer. This way you can use your hard-earned cash on recording yourself, rather than spending thousands of dollars in someone else's studio. Even after you have spent money for studio time, you will still need to get your material mixed, mastered, get graphics done and get CDs pressed. Not only can a powerful computer do all this, but you will also be in control of your own recording. As a result, you can start a new project whenever you want, without having the expense of to go back into someone else's studio.

A virtual studio can consist of as little as a computer, guitars, amp and a microphone.

PROS AND CONS OF VIRTUAL STUDIOS

One of the reasons many musicians are opting to build virtual studios is how compact they are. If you have very little space for a studio where you live, going virtual may be the answer. Your equipment can start out with a computer, keyboard (MIDI controller), speakers and, of course, your guitars. All of this can fit almost unnoticed into a corner of a room. The other huge motivation is that all of the hardware is replaced by software, which tends to cost less. You can even download various types of software from the Internet or get programs free from companies promoting their products.

Another advantage to the virtual approach is having fewer worries about troubleshooting your equipment. The more external gear you own, the more likely it is something will malfunction. You can waste a lot of time, for example, just trying to figure out why you can't get a signal from an effect, and have to locate exactly where the problem is coming from. Also, expensive gear that you purchase can become obsolete in as little as a year or sooner, while in virtual land you can upgrade your software for little or no cost.

An amazing tool found in virtual studios is the ability to automate the work that you do, including panning, volumes, effects, etc. This saves a lot of time and frustration since you don't have to start from scratch every time you record. If the parameters of your reverb are set a certain way in the evening, you can save them so when you return the next morning they will be exactly the same.

Suffice it to say that there are many advantages to virtual studios, but there are disadvantages as well. For one, there is a big learning curve when it comes to properly running new software. You will also need a powerful computer to start with and upgrades may not be compatible with your present capabilities. Some computers, even if they are state-of-the-art, may not be upgradeable and you may need a replacement. Computers still have glitches, especially when running a few programs at the same time. The digital domain can also give your guitar a cold sound, although you can still mic your guitars or use a preamp. You will also be using MIDI to access certain virtual sounds, which will require either a keyboard or guitar MIDI controller. The keyboard controller is the most popular choice, but if you don't play keyboard there would also be a learning curve there. Guitar controllers offer a bit more freedom of movement, although they are difficult to move around without banging into something, while keyboards are stationary.

All in all, more musicians are progressing into the virtual world all the time, and as technology advances, we are bound to see some great things happen in this realm.

WHAT YOU WILL NEED

COMPUTER

If you already own a computer, you will need to make sure there is enough memory and hard drive space to support a virtual studio. Because of the ever-increasing demands of software and its capabilities, you will need the utmost speed and memory available. Most software will let you know its minimum requirements on the packaging. The right amount of speed and memory will allow your computer to run smoothly.

The one question that arises in purchasing a new computer is "Should I buy a Mac or a PC?" A lot of it will depend on what computer you are presently used to. Both will produce good results, just keep in mind that there are variations of both.

HARD DRIVE

Be sure that the hard drive in your computer is fast enough to accommodate all the information it will process. If it is not, you will need to add another hard drive for all your virtual applications. Any virtual studio that has over 32 tracks will need an extra hard drive. You could have it installed internally or it could be external hardware. If you don't have the right devices to connect anything externally, you will need to get an adapter card installed. An example of this is an ISA expansion card. Instructions on installation of these cards are included when you purchase them. If you don't want to go through the hassle of adding extras to your computer, you can purchase a computer made for audio applications. Be sure to let the retailers know exactly what you are planning to do.

THE SOUNDCARD

Soundcards work in conjunction with the digital audio sequencer in your computer. Also called audio cards, they convert analog into digital information and/or vice versa. Most computers come with stock cards when you purchase them, but you will want to upgrade your card for a more professional one. Not only do the upgraded soundcards produce a superior quality sound, but they also have many more inputs and outputs, with an assortment of digital connections.

Technical Tip No. 28—Extra Disk Drives

Consider adding a second hard drive just for your studio. Your primary drive should contain all your programs plus your operating system (Windows, Mac OSX, etc.). Your secondary drive is where you would store audio samples, such as drum loops. You could even have a third drive to store all your recorded work. The advantage of having more than one drive is the ability to keep everything organized. Also, if one of your drives ever crashed, you would be able to salvage what was on the other drive(s).

If you already have a computer for recording, be sure that any soundcard you buy is compatible with the motherboard. If you don't presently own a computer or need to get a more powerful one, spend some time researching what kind of soundcard you want to buy and then get your computer custom built around it.

MIDI Interface

Your MIDI card or MIDI interface can be internal or external. It allows your MIDI controller (keyboard or guitar) to interact with your computer software/sequencer. At this writing, the standard external MIDI interface has 16 channels. If you require more than 16, you will need a more advanced interface. Some controllers are capable of interacting directly with your computer, eliminating the need for a separate interface. Many controllers have their own output port (such as a USB port) which connects to the computer. This allows you to bypass an external MIDI interface.

Plug-Ins

Plug-ins are software-based virtual effects used to process your recorded data, such as adding reverb. Depending on how many effect plug-ins are being used at the same time, they require more processing power (this is another reason to have a powerful computer). You will need to install these plug-ins just like regular software.

Plug-ins are categorized either as effects or instruments. Effects include reverb, EQ, compression, etc. Instruments might be drum sounds, keyboards, strings and so on.

MIDI Controller

MIDI devices such as a keyboard, guitar or drums allow the user to write/program music into the computer's sequencer/software. Some controllers, like most keyboard controllers, have built-in sounds and can also act as the sound source. If you have a controller that does not have internal sounds, you will have to rely on externa l sound modules, other keyboards or virtual instruments (software-based sounds).

Technical Tip No. 29—The Soundcard

It's a good idea that before you purchase an upgraded soundcard that you decide how many tracks you will be utilizing simultaneously. Some soundcards will not allow you to record more than two tracks at a time, although it is becoming easier to get soundcards that do. It's best to double check before you purchase.

Many guitar players own keyboards as part of their virtual studios. This is because the evolution of the virtual studio was based mostly upon synthesizer sounds and their applications.

Mixing and Mastering
You can obtain software that will let you mix and master your own songs. For demos this is okay, but you may still consider bringing it to a professional if you plan on shopping your product to a label or distributing you own CD.

HOW TO RECORD A SONG ON YOUR COMPUTER
The following are some suggestions on how to get started recording a song on your computer.

1. **First Choose the Instrumentation**
   Decide if you are going to use real or virtual instruments or a combination. For virtual instruments, decide if you want samples or grooves. If you are using real instruments, like your guitar or your voice, you may have to use microphones.

2. **Bed Tracks**
   Once you have mapped out your instrumentation, you will need to lay down your bed tracks. These refer to the foundational tracks of your song, such as drums and bass. For drums, you may choose to use imported loops. Once you find a loop that will work, you can copy and paste the loop so it is repeated throughout the song. For variety, you can add a few different loops at different sections, such as at your chorus or at the bridge. Some people sequence entire drum parts with a drum machine (just another MIDI controller). After you've laid down your drums, then try adding bass lines. If you are playing a real bass, you can record directly into the computer (adding some processing effects if so desired) or you can access a module bass patch, using your MIDI controller to play the part. The magic of virtual recording is you don't have to play the whole song. If you have three choruses, you can record your bass line once and then copy and paste it into the other choruses. Keep in mind, though, that copying parts can take away the human feel of a song, so you may want to be selective about how many times you copy the same part.

Technical Tip No. 30—MIDI Controllers

When purchasing a keyboard MIDI controller, some of the features to look for are how many notes it has, pitch-bend and aftertouch (the ability to sense the amount of pressure which is being applied to the keys while they are depressed. This information may be used to control some aspects of the sound produced by the synthesizer—vibrato, for example). These features allow you to alter the sounds, adding authenticity to certain sampled instruments.

---

3. **Rhythm and Lead Tracks**

   Now that your drums and bass are recorded, you have a good idea of the feel of your tune. Your guitar tracks could be recorded next. This is where it gets fun because you can experiment with your ideas. In virtual recording, you're not on the clock! Record a few tracks of your guitar rhythm and then decide which ones you would like to keep. Another great experiment is to try applying different effects to the guitar tracks and see if you come up with something you like.

4. **Vocal Tracks**

   Of course, you will need to use a microphone in order to get your voice into the computer. It's a good idea to invest in some preamp software to warm up the voice. The computer is not as forgiving on vocals as it is for other instruments. You can dress up guitar and bass with effects, but you can only add so much to cover up weak vocals. The most common problem with vocalists is intonation. To get better results with your pitch, take one headphone off an ear so you don't only hear head tones. If you have real pitch problems, invest in pitch correction software (there are several available). Be careful, this software can only help so much and if it is overused it will end up sounding like an effect.

5. **Other Instruments**

   To make your arrangements interesting, try adding other instruments, such as organ or keyboard pads and synthesizer sounds. There are also sampled solo lines available for computer, such as horn lines, backup vocals, and so on.

There is a lot to learn when it comes to going virtual, but if you view your career as a studio musician as something you are in for the long haul, it makes it a little easier. Just learn a little bit at a time and the next thing you know, you'll be very knowledgeable. Keep a network of people you can call to help you for troubleshooting and technical support. The main thing to remember is to have fun, stay creative and don't get too caught up in all the technical stuff.

CHAPTER 9
RECORDING YOUR INSTRUMENTS

On page 71, we looked at recording direct. You can also mic your instrument. Some processors used in software can sound too digital or have an over-processed sound. Unless you've got state-of-the-art digital gear, you are probably better off learning how to get authentic recordings with a microphone.

MICROPHONES 101

To use microphones correctly, you should have at least a basic understanding of how they work. A mic takes acoustic energy (sound) and converts it into an electronic signal. Using a mic to record your equipment (be it guitar, vocals or even drums) isn't rocket science, but there are a few important things to know.

RESPONSE PATTERNS

It is important to be aware of the response patterns of your microphone. Simply put, a microphone will pick up frequencies that are projected toward it from a certain area within a 360-degree radius from itself. The three main types of responses are:

- **Omnidirectional**: Will record sound coming from any direction (good when you want to capture the ambience of a room).

- **Bidirectional**: Records sound waves from its front and back.

- **Directional**: Receives the signal only from the area that it is pointed toward (good for recording amps).

DYNAMIC VS. CONDENSER MICROPHONES

There are two types of microphones: dynamic and condenser.

DYNAMIC MICROPHONES

These mics are used for recording as well as live performances. They are quite durable and respond very well to the source (the sound you are recording). You can purchase them inexpensively and if you buy a used one, it can be downright cheap. As of this writing, the industry standard for some time has been the Shure SM57 for instruments and SM58 for vocals. There are other brands that are just as good but you need to check them out to make sure they are well constructed. Most music stores have new and used dynamic mics that you can try out. If you inform them of what you are looking for, you should be able to find something to suit your budget.

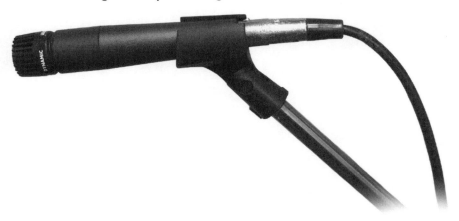

Dynamic microphones are the industry standard and very popular for live
performances as well as recording instruments in the studio.

CONDENSER MICROPHONES

These microphones, also called capacitor mics, are great for the studio. They tend to be more expensive than dynamic mics but the costs keep coming down. Some condenser microphones have the technology to duplicate the response of tubes and can cost thousands of dollars.

Condenser mics work well if you are recording vocals or acoustic guitars, since they are highly sensitive and generate a powerful signal. They can even pick up sounds going on in another room, such as a telephone ringing or people speaking. These mics also pick up the sounds of humming from any electronic sources, so you will need a fairly quiet environment for recording.

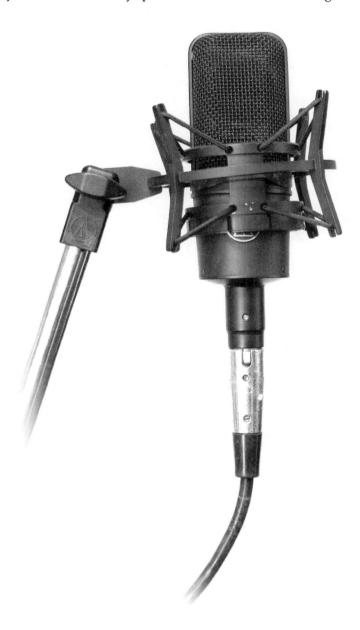

Condenser microphones are known for their extreme sensitivity and broad frequency response, which can be up to 20kHz, or more.

Technical Tip No. 31—Mic Technique

To develop your understanding of microphones, plug one into a P.A. (public address system) and practice speaking into it. This will help you understand how it responds. A dynamic mic will be sensitive to where you position the mic in relation to your mouth. A condenser mic will still pickup your voice, even if you move a foot or so away. You will also discover that with a dynamic mic, if you sing too loud or too close to it, it can actually distort. This also applies to recording your amplifier and will determine the proximity of your mic to the speaker.

MIC TECHNIQUES

Now that you have some foundational knowledge of how microphones work, let's discuss how to apply it in your home studio.

ACOUSTIC GUITARS

Acoustic guitars include classical and steel-string acoustics, as well as 12-string guitars—any guitar that doesn't plug into an amp. Acoustic guitars have very extensive dynamics, which can range from loud rock strumming to a very soft, folky, fingerstyle picking. Because of this, a condenser microphone is the proper choice. If you only own a dynamic mic, you can use it but it will be a little trickier.

Try using two microphones to achieve a stereo effect or to catch some of the ambience of the room. Put one mic where the neck joins the body and the other mic closer to the soundhole, but not too close to it. The closer a mic is to the soundhole, the warmer it will sound. Experiment with different placements to see what sounds the most natural. Each of these mics will be running into its own line in the mixer. You can then pan them left and right and decide later at what ratio you want to mix them.

PHASE CANCELLATION

Phase cancellation can occur when more than one mic is being used for recording in a room. When the mic wave forms get mixed they can become out-of-phase, altering the sound of what is being recorded. For instance, if you are micing an instrument but find that adding an extra mic changes the EQ (some of the bass or treble drops out), it is the result of phase cancellation. Although some engineers use this effect on purpose, most of the time it is undesireable. You can solve this problem by either changing the polarity on one of your mics or moving the mic to a different spot in the room.

> **Technical Tip No. 32—Mic Placement**
>
> *A common mistake that novices make when recording an acoustic guitar is to put their microphone close to the guitar soundhole. Many guitarists incorrectly assume the sound "comes from" the soundhole, but this is untrue. While most luthiers believe a soundhole enhances the volume and tone of an acoustic guitar, it is the vibrating top that is responsible for most of the sound. So although it may seem logical to put a mic in front of the soundhole, this placement will create a boxy, boomy sound. The best place to position a condenser microphone is where the neck and the body meet, 12 to 18 inches away from the guitar. A dynamic mic should be placed in front of the same spot, but very close to the guitar.*

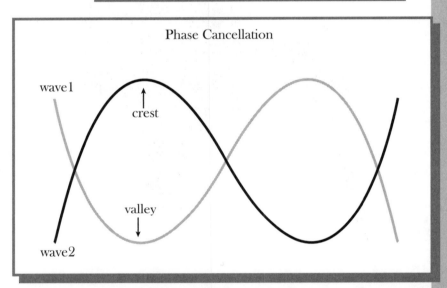

Think of each sound wave as having a crest and a valley (high point and low point). If the crest of one wave is aligned with the valley of another, the two sound waves interfere with one another and the sound is affected.

Place your microphone where the neck joins the body. You can move it towards the soundhole for a warmer tone or away from the soundhole for a brighter tone.

HOW TO MIC AMPS FOR ELECTRIC GUITARS

For decades, dynamic microphones such as the Shure SM57 have been popular for recording amps. If you only have one mic, you can get pretty good results if this is the type you have. You'll get good results specifically on smaller amps with open backs with only one speaker. Point your microphone on an angle towards the center of the speaker (this is called close micing). This will get a fairly bright sound. If you want a warmer sound, move the microphone closer to the cone of the speaker. To generate an even warmer tone, you can place an additional mic behind the amp. Once again, you will need to experiment to see what sounds best to you.

Another popular technique is to combine two microphones: one close mic and the other for ambiance. For an ambience mic, you can use an omnidirectional condenser mic positioned on a boom stand facing the amp from several feet away. You can then mix both signals to create a more realistic sound.

Dynamic mics are a good choice for close micing. The mic should be anywhere from one to six inches away from the amp.

Omnidirectional condenser mics can pick up the ambience from your room and add natural color when blended with close micing.

To get a good sound from your amp, you will need to have it turned up fairly loud. This can be quite a problem if you have to record in the same room as your amp.

You can solve this dilemma by isolating your amp in another room. Since most musicians only have one room to work with, the best situation is to put it in the closet. As long as there is enough space around the amp (so it won't overheat) you should get a pretty good sound. Of course, this will only work for close micing. If you don't have a closet available, build a square box from plywood that your amp will fit into, leaving about a foot all around the amp. You can cut a hole in the back for air to come through and use a fan if it gets too hot. Put thick fabric, preferably carpet around the box to help mute some of the sound. For very loud volumes, elevate the amp off of the floor to isolate the sound from any people underneath you.

HOW TO MIC A DRUMSET

If you are also going to be recording a live bass track you don't need to worry about microphones, since it works just fine to record bass tracks direct to the mixer. But here are a few suggestions for recording live drum tracks.

1. Use a dynamic mic for the snare, positioned above it and pointing down towards it.

2. Put a dynamic mic on a short boom stand inside the kick drum, about 6 inches from the inside of the drum head.

3. Use two ominidirectional condenser mics on boom stands overhead, facing the drum kit five feet apart from one another.

You don't need any more mics, since your overheads will catch the crash cymbals as well as the toms. If you rarely record drums, consider renting these additional microphones from your local music store instead of buying them.

HOW TO MIC VOCALS

Although recording vocals is quite straightforward, it is very easy for a vocal track to sound unprofessional. The most common mistake is using the incorrect microphone. If you are recording yourself or the lead vocalist in your band, be sure to invest the proper amount of time and locate the microphone best suited for vocals. Just because a mic is expensive, it is not necessarily going to produce the best results. Each human voice is very unique, which explains why there are a myriad mics on the market.

Most performing vocalists will use a dynamic mic for their live shows since they work well for diction and treble boost. For the studio, though, it is best to use a condenser microphone, which has a wider frequency response. Condenser mics amplify the sibilance ("s" sounds) in vocalists because of their wide frequency response.

Pop shields are popular for recording vocalists. They deflect any popping noises coming from the vocalists when they use "P" or "S" in their words. You can make your own by taking a clothes hanger and creating a circle about four to six inches in diameter and then stretching a piece of pantyhose over the front of it. See picture below.

Pop shields are used to avert vocal popping sounds.

Another common problem with recording vocals is singing too close to the mic. The vocalist should stand anywhere from six inches up to two feet from the mic for the best results. Keep the mic away from the walls in your room to avoid unnecessary echo (reflections off the walls). If you need to make the room more dead, add some extra curtains or carpet.

> ### *Technical Tip No. 34—Headphone Monitoring*
>
> *In order for a vocalist to hear the music while recording only voice, headphones are used. Fully-enclosed headphones work the best since there is little bleed (sound that escapes the headphones) that will be picked up by the microphone.*

Compression is also an important element when recording the human voice. It will stop the vocals from sounding like they are jumping out of the mix, especially if the vocalist has a very dynamic voice. You will want to add just enough compression to control dynamics but not completely cut off the top or bottom end of the voice. Too much compression will ruin the naturalness of the track. It is always better to use less during recording, and add more at mixdown if needed.

CHAPTER 10
PRODUCING A PROFESSIONAL DEMO

Long gone are the days when you could just put together a cassette tape and a J-card for the cassette case to promote your music. Today, people (musician and non-musician alike) have higher standards and expect demos to be presented very professionally.

CD demos have become the norm and many of them have studio-quality production. Those that put just anything together regardless of the quality of music or visual production, hoping people will be able to see through to their talent, rarely get very far. Graphics software such as Adobe Photoshop or Microsoft Photo Editor have become more and more user friendly. At the same time, recording software like Cubase or Cakewalk are standard in the industry. Most new computers come already equipped with a CD writer. Combined, all of this has raised the bar with regard to demo production. Even young teenagers who have access to computers at home or at school are coming up with some impressive material. Of course, that doesn't mean that every demo out there is up to par. Unfortunately, there are still a lot of very unprofessional demos being produced. All in all, however, people are becoming more aware of the importance of image and professional sound.

If that seems a little discouraging to you because you don't have a big budget or don't know too much about how to put a polished demo together, you just need to view it like everything else. There is a learning curve when it comes to producing a great demo and it takes patience and will-power to bring it to fruition.

1. IDENTIFY YOUR MARKET

The first thing to figure out is to whom you are marketing your demo. Every market has different demands, so you need to zero in on the expectations. For example, if you are putting together a demo to find gigs in local bars, your approach should be different than if you are sending a demo to a record company. Generally, most bars, unless they are an establishment that specifically supports original music, will want to hear a demo with cover tunes. Also, if the bar books mostly R&B acts but you have an alternative rock band, there is a chance that you are just wasting your time and efforts giving them your material.

On the other hand, if you are shopping around for a record deal, you will absolutely want to have original tunes on your demo. A good practice is to have your first song as a cover tune—one you play really well—which will help warm up the A&R executives to your sound. A&R refers to artist and repertoire people, a term coined to describe the function of people at record labels who are in charge of finding and developing new talent.

Young artists will often send a demo which includes anywhere from seven to ten tunes. That is not a demo. That is a full CD. People receiving your demo don't want to hear 10 tunes, especially busy A&R executives or bar owners. Not only do they not have the time, but as a rule, they've made up their mind within the first song or two whether or not they are interested in your music.

Another thing to consider is that playing all the licks and techniques you know to impress people may actually work against you. Your mentality needs to be that your guitar parts are there to enhance the songs and not necessarily to showcase everything you've got. Overplaying on a tune would make it appear that you are trying too hard or are not mature enough in your craft to know when to lay back. Even if you are sending a demo to a bandleader to do sub work, or to be a part of the band, you don't want to look like a solo hog. If the listener thinks all you are concerned about is showing off your great talent, they may be concerned that attitude will transfer to a band situation.

Choose three or four of your best tunes showcasing various aspects of your playing. One tune could simply be rhythm guitar with some of your favorite effects. Another could be to demonstrate your technique and ability to improvise. If you're playing behind a vocalist, make sure that you have them louder than yourself in the mix. If you also sing backup or lead, be sure to add that to your recording since a bandleader will often consider it a bonus.

Even an independent, self-produced CD package
can be very professional in appearance.

2. CONCENTRATE ON GOOD QUALITY, NOT TECHNOLOGY

When you are producing any recording in the studio, it is too easy to get lost in all the technical aspects. For example, you can spend a whole lot of time just focusing on getting the perfect reverb for your mix, or mastering everything to perfection. These things may be important, but keep in mind that a demo is only the introduction to your talent and musical style. You need to focus on presenting great tunes and tastefully showcasing your music chops. The listener is looking to hear the overall feel of the songs and how well you play them. Unless they are an engineer or producer, a lot of the technological tricks you spent so much time on will go right over their heads.

3. ANALYZE OTHER DEMOS

A good exercise is to get a hold of other demos and compare them to yours. It's a great way to learn what to do and what not to do. If you have friends who work in venues such as bars, see if they'll let you listen to the demos that come in. The best situation is if you know someone who would be willing to lend or give you some CDs that have been discarded (that happens often).

Another helpful thing is to join one of your local festival committees and do some volunteer work. If you have any office experience, this is one way to get into their office, where you can quietly check out the materials that are coming in. Festivals get hundreds to thousands of promotional kits every year. They run the gamut, from very poorly produced graphics and production to extremely professional promotional packages which include video, demos, posters and media clippings.

You may even let the festival organizers know that you are producing your own demo and, once they are done with the packages, you would like to keep some to help in your endeavors. They may view that as their opportunity to help your career.

If there is a panel of judges who decide who gets chosen for these festivals and who gets the boot, ask them how they arrive at their decisions. This is a very useful piece of information, since many of the people who make decisions are not musicians. They may have an entirely different agenda in mind, and base their decisions on issues not related to musical quality, such as "we don't need any more blues players this year." Sometimes, getting the inside scoop can help you understand why your CD may go unnoticed, even if it is an extremely good recording. Too often in the music business, the powers that be have much different goals than musicians. Usually we have little control over this situation, but the more knowledge you have of how things are run, the more you can prepare yourself for success.

4. IMAGE IS EVERYTHING

Image or perception is everything; as cliché as that may sound, in the entertainment/music market, it is the absolute truth. You may have the greatest demo mankind has ever produced but if you present a shoddy looking CD, you will not be taken seriously. And if you think the bar owner down the street doesn't know the difference—he does. There are many great musicians competing for just a few gigs. You need to make a good first impression.

There are many graphic programs available, so there is no excuse for poor packaging. Of course, there is a learning curve before you can smoothly maneuver through any software. If you are in this business for the long haul, take the attitude that this is important education. One can not depend on musical talent alone and expect to be simply "discovered." This attitude doesn't work as well as it used to. More and more guitarists are getting their business and image chops together without feeling they are compromising. This is your competition.

If you don't want to learn how to operate graphic software, be prepared to dish out some cash for someone else to do it for you. This can be costly, especially if you tend to be picky about what you want. Graphic shops tend to have a more generic approach, so you may have to settle for a more basic design. If you have a buddy who will do it for you, that is great, but you may not want to impose every time you make a new CD, or need to make necessary adjustments on your CD labels. You could ask your friend to give you a crash course and give you technical support as you learn some of the more challenging aspects of the software.

Local R&B band demo used for booking gigs and festivals.

Another demo CD for a hip-hop, R&B band used for getting local gigs.

5. WWW.DONTFORGETTHEWEB

The Internet has turned out to be a great, inexpensive tool for self promotion. It is becoming standard for people to ask musicians for their Web page addresses. There are many things you can't control in the music industry, but this is one area in which you have total control over the impression you make.

There are two ways you can handle your Website. The expensive way is hiring someone to do it for you. It is much less expensive to do it yourself. A Website can be as costly as you want it to be. If money isn't a problem, you can hire a graphic artist to do the art work for you, which usually gets great results. They could also update any information or graphics as needed, which the person you hired could teach you to do.

Not only can you put your demo online or snippets from your upcoming CD, you can put listings of upcoming gigs, news clippings, articles or any other thing that might promote your talent. People can download video or live footage of one of your concerts. Another great tool is to offer guitar lessons and give expert advice in your field. Always keep a digital camera on hand to take pictures of events or people you can add to your site. The sky is the limit and all of these features help in giving the impression that you are a pro and have good business skills.

Many ambitious musicians own directories listing record companies, radio stations and various industry people. These directories are useful guides for sending out promotional material. You may find such directories at your local music store or at big chain bookstores. If you do plan on sending material to music executives through the Internet, you may want to be selective and limit the amount of material you send. It is customary to ask permission before sending them anything.

If your Web site has a calendar listing your gigs, be sure to keep it up to date. It gives a bad impression if your last listing was eight months ago and there haven't been any new listings since. It gives the impression that you disappeared off the market or, worse, that you are not taking care of business.

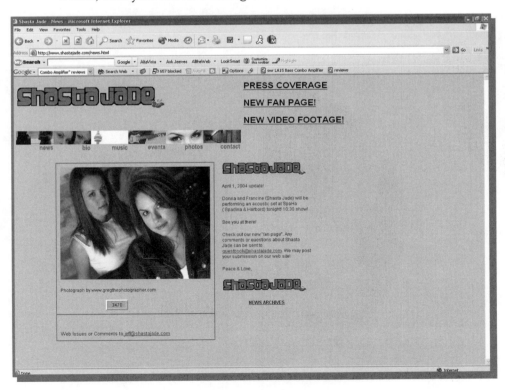

A well-produced website makes a good impression. It's good to update it frequently,
so that fans can find something new each time they visit.